ISSUES IN INTERNATIONAL TAXATION

No. 6

The Application of the OECD Model Tax Convention to Partnerships

ORGANISATION FOR ECONOMIC CO-OPERATION AND DEVELOPMENT

ORGANISATION FOR ECONOMIC CO-OPERATION AND DEVELOPMENT

Pursuant to Article 1 of the Convention signed in Paris on 14th December 1960, and which came into force on 30th September 1961, the Organisation for Economic Co-operation and Development (OECD) shall promote policies designed:
- to achieve the highest sustainable economic growth and employment and a rising standard of living in Member countries, while maintaining financial stability, and thus to contribute to the development of the world economy;
- to contribute to sound economic expansion in Member as well as non-member countries in the process of economic development; and
- to contribute to the expansion of world trade on a multilateral, non-discriminatory basis in accordance with international obligations.

The original Member countries of the OECD are Austria, Belgium, Canada, Denmark, France, Germany, Greece, Iceland, Ireland, Italy, Luxembourg, the Netherlands, Norway, Portugal, Spain, Sweden, Switzerland, Turkey, the United Kingdom and the United States. The following countries became Members subsequently through accession at the dates indicated hereafter: Japan (28th April 1964), Finland (28th January 1969), Australia (7th June 1971), New Zealand (29th May 1973), Mexico (18th May 1994), the Czech Republic (21st December 1995), Hungary (7th May 1996), Poland (22nd November 1996) and Korea (12th December 1996). The Commission of the European Communities takes part in the work of the OECD (Article 13 of the OECD Convention).

Publié en français sous le titre :
L'application du Modèle de Convention fiscale de l'OCDE aux sociétés de personnes

© OECD 1999
Permission to reproduce a portion of this work for non-commercial purposes or classroom use should be obtained through the Centre français d'exploitation du droit de copie (CFC), 20, rue des Grands-Augustins, 75006 Paris, France, Tel. (33-1) 44 07 47 70, Fax (33-1) 46 34 67 19, for every country except the United States. In the United States permission should be obtained through the Copyright Clearance Center, Customer Service, (508)750-8400, 222 Rosewood Drive, Danvers, MA 01923 USA, or CCC Online. http://www.copyright.com/. All other applications for permission to reproduce or translate all or part of this book should be made to OECD Publications, 2, rue André-Pascal, 75775 Paris Cedex 16, France.

FOREWORD

This publication, the sixth in the series "Issues in International Taxation", includes the report entitled "The Application of the OECD Model Tax Convention to Partnerships" which the Committee on Fiscal Affairs adopted, and decided to make available to the public, on 20 January 1999.

The report deals with the application of the provisions of the OECD Model Tax Convention, and indirectly of bilateral tax conventions based on that Model, to partnerships. It puts forward a number of changes to the Model Tax Convention which will be included in the next update to the Model.

At the time of adopting the report, the delegations for France, Germany, the Netherlands, Portugal and Switzerland have expressed reservations on various aspects of it. These reservations are reproduced in Annex II.

TABLE OF CONTENTS

I. INTRODUCTION 7
    I.1   Background 7
    I.2   Organisation of the report 7

II. APPLICATION OF TAX CONVENTIONS BY THE STATE OF SOURCE ... 9
    II.1   Preliminary remarks on the tax treatment of foreign entities 9
    II.2   Differences that affect the tax treatment of partnerships........................... 10
    II.3   When is a partnership entitled to the benefits of a tax convention?........... 12
    II.4   The partners' entitlement to treaty benefits when the partnership
          is not a resident... 17
    II.5   Entitlement to treaty benefits when one State treats the partnership
          as a taxable entity.. 23
    II.6   Application of the Convention where the benefits are dependent upon
          certain characteristics or attributes of the taxpayer 31

III. APPLICATION OF TAX CONVENTIONS BY THE STATE OF
     RESIDENCE... 35
    III.1 Conflicts of qualification.. 36
    III.2 Problems arising from conflicts of income allocation 44

ANNEX I: PROPOSED CHANGES TO THE OECD MODEL TAX
              CONVENTION.. 51

    Articles of the Model.. 51
    Commentary 51

ANNEX II: RESERVATIONS 63

    France 63
    Germany.. 65
    The Netherlands 66
    Portugal... 67
    Switzerland 68

ANNEX III: LIST OF ENTITIES IN SELECTED COUNTRIES 69

THE APPLICATION OF THE OECD MODEL TAX CONVENTION TO PARTNERSHIPS

I. INTRODUCTION

I.1 Background

1. In 1993, the Committee formed a Working Group to study the application of the Model Tax Convention to partnerships, trusts, and other non-corporate entities. This first report by the Working Group, which the Committee adopted on 20 January 1999, focuses exclusively on partnerships. The Committee recognises, however, that many of the principles discussed in its report may also apply with respect to other non-corporate entities and therefore intends to now examine the application of the Model Tax Convention to these other entities in light of this report.

2. In this respect, it should also be noted that the references to "partnerships" in this report cover entities that qualify as such under civil or commercial law as opposed to tax law. Thus the term "partnership", as used in this report, does not imply anything about the tax treatment of the relevant entity and should not be confused with a reference to entities, whether partnerships or not, which are treated as transparent for tax purposes.

3. At the beginning of the work on this topic, it was decided that this work should generally focus on practical cases and an approach based on the discussion of factual examples was therefore adopted. It was quickly found that many of the problems that were brought to the attention of the Committee arose from so-called "conflicts of qualification" — cases where the treaty partners interpret or apply the treaty in different ways. The Committee agreed that while this broader issue extended beyond the treatment of partnerships under tax conventions, it should nevertheless be dealt with in the context of this work on partnerships.

I.2 Organisation of the report

4. As previously indicated, this report focuses on specific factual examples. For each example, the facts and, where applicable, relevant aspects of domestic tax laws are described. The Committee's analysis of how the OECD Model Tax Convention applies

in the example is then presented and, where appropriate, changes to the Model Tax Convention are put forward.

5. Section II discusses various aspects of the application of tax conventions by the State of source where partnerships are involved. It includes a discussion of the entitlement to treaty benefits of partners and partnerships in various circumstances.

6. Section III addresses issues arising from the application of tax conventions by the State of residence. Subsection III.1 discusses problems related to conflicts of qualification while subsection III.2 discusses problems related to conflicts of income allocation.

7. Annex I includes changes to the Model Tax Convention which are either specifically included in the report or reflect its contents. Annex II includes general observations by France, Germany, the Netherlands, Portugal and Switzerland. Annex III includes a list of entities found in the countries that have co-operated to the preparation of this report.

8. The following abbreviations are used in this report:

    P   =   The partnership

    A and B =   Partners in P

    State P = The State in which P is located

    State R = The State of residence of one or all the partners

    State S = The State of source, i.e. the State in which income arises, where three States are involved

9. Similarly, the following symbols are used in the various diagrams used in this report:

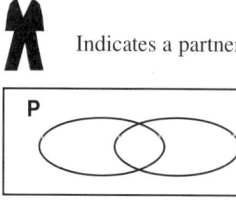
Indicates a partner of partnership P

Indicates a company

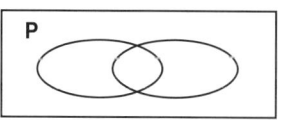
Indicates the partnership

Indicates that the State treats partnerships as transparent entities

Indicates a fixed base or permanent establishment

Indicates that the State treats partnerships as taxable entities

APPLICATION OF THE MODEL TAX CONVENTION TO PARTNERSHIPS

II. APPLICATION OF TAX CONVENTIONS BY THE STATE OF SOURCE

II.1 *Preliminary remarks on the tax treatment of foreign entities*

10. In addressing the issue of how tax conventions apply to partnerships, a useful starting point is to examine how foreign entities are treated for purposes of the taxation, by the State of source, of income derived from its territory.

11. In most Member countries, as a matter of principle, tax laws apply on the basis of the legal relationship deriving from other branches of the law. Thus the tax laws of these countries, when referring to partnerships, will, absent special tax definitions, refer to those entities that constitute partnerships according to domestic civil or commercial law.

12. Difficulties often arise, however, where income is derived by an entity organised under the laws of another jurisdiction. In that case, the entity will have to be classified for purposes of the application of the tax laws of the country where the income is derived, regardless of whether or not that classification is compatible with the civil or commercial law system of the jurisdiction from which the entity derives its legal status.

13. For example, if the tax system of a country recognises only individuals, companies and partnerships (but not trusts) as taxpayers and provides for a different tax treatment for these three types of taxpayers, that country will have to "force" foreign entities in one or the other of these categories (with more or less difficulty depending on the similarity of the civil and commercial law of the countries concerned) for purposes of applying its tax system to domestic income derived by these foreign entities.

14. In doing so, the practice of most countries is to adopt the same approach as the one they apply in a purely domestic context. They will therefore apply their domestic tax classification to foreign entities on the basis of the foreign law's legal characteristics of the entity. In the previous example, the country, for the purposes of taxing the domestic income of a trust established under the law of a foreign jurisdiction, will typically examine the legal characteristics of the trust as they derive from the trust law of the foreign jurisdiction in order to determine whom it should tax and whether that person should be taxed as an individual, company or partnership, which are the only categories recognised under its tax law.

15. In a system of international taxation where income taxes are levied on the basis of both residence and source, this means that, in addition to the well-known problem of the same item of income being taxed in the State of residence and the State of source, there will be risks of double-taxation or non-taxation associated with:

- the different classification of a given entity in the State of residence and the State of source,

– the different tax treatment, in these States, of a given entity despite common classification.

These risks, which are further analysed in the next two subsections, are compounded when the participants in the entity (e.g. the partners of a partnership) reside in a different State from that in which the entity has been established. Subsection II.2 discusses how these differences are particularly important for partnerships.

II.2   *Differences that affect the tax treatment of partnerships*

a)   Different classification

16.   While most, if not all, Member countries recognise the concepts of company and of partnership for tax purposes, their definitions of these two concepts may vary.

17.   In most cases, the similarities between the legal systems of the Member countries will be sufficient to ensure that what is a company or a partnership in the country where it has been established is recognised as such, for tax purposes, in other countries. Entities, however, that are not widespread in the civil or commercial laws of the Member countries will create difficulties if they cannot easily be classified in one of these categories but need to be so classified for tax purposes. In that case, it is possible that one country will treat the entity as a partnership while the other will treat it as a company, with completely different tax results.

b)   Different treatment

18.   Problems will also arise, however, where two countries classify a given entity in the same way but treat that entity in different ways.

19.   These problems are particularly important for partnerships and most of the examples in this report are based on these problems. A well-known difficulty is that while some countries treat partnerships as transparent entities, imposing no tax on the partnership itself but taxing each partners on its share of the partnership's income, others treat the partnership as a taxable entity, usually taxing the partnership on its income as if it were a company.

20.   There are, however, many other possible differences which may result in double taxation or non-taxation, some of which are discussed in this report. For instance, while some countries accept that a partner may also be a creditor of the partnership and may therefore derive interest income from the partnership, others consider that no interest may be paid to a partner, any payment of what purports to be interest being treated as a distribution of the income of the partnership.

APPLICATION OF THE MODEL TAX CONVENTION TO PARTNERSHIPS

21. Other differences relate to how countries apply the transparency approach. The mere fact that the income of the partnership is taxed at the partners' level does not, in itself, address all issues related to the computation of the tax to be paid on that income. Tax rules often differ depending on the nature of the taxpayer or on the relationship between the taxpayer and another party to a transaction. Countries may have different views as to what extent the partnership should be ignored in applying rules based on the nature of the taxpayer or on its relationship with another person (the question of the extent to which a transparent partnership should be ignored for the purposes of the application of the provisions of tax conventions is discussed in subsection II.6 below).

22. To assist countries in identifying cases where these differences may create problems, the Committee has decided to develop a list that describes the tax treatment of entities established under the laws of each country and commonly used for commercial and investment purposes. That list is included in Annex III.

c)   The effect on tax conventions

23. The differences described above create a number of difficulties with respect to the application of the provisions of tax conventions.

24. The Commentary on Article 1 of the Model Tax Convention already refers to the problem described in paragraph 19 above in the following words:

> "The domestic laws of the various OECD Member countries differ in the treatment of partnerships. The main issue of such differences is founded on the fact that some countries treat partnerships as taxable units (sometimes even as companies) whereas other countries disregard the partnership and tax only the individual partners on their share of the partnership income."

25. The difficulties that this and other differences create in the context of the application of the provisions of tax conventions are discussed throughout this report. This section focuses on the problems that the differences described above create for the application of the Convention by the State of source, including the determination of who is entitled to the benefits of a tax convention in relation to income derived by a partnership (subsections II.3 to II.5) and the application of the provisions of the Convention that are dependent upon certain characteristics or attributes of the taxpayer (subsection II.6). Section III deals with the problems related to the application of the Convention by the State of residence, focusing on conflicts of qualification (subsection III.1) and conflicts of income allocation (subsection III.2).

26. The Committee believes that many of these difficulties may be solved through a better co-ordination in the application and interpretation of some of the provisions of tax conventions. This report puts forwards a number of suggestions in that respect.

II.3 When is a partnership entitled to the benefits of a tax convention?

27. Where income is derived from a particular State, the determination of the tax consequences in that State will first require the application of the domestic tax laws of that State. It is the provisions of these laws that will determine who may be subjected to tax on that income in that State. The provisions of tax conventions, however, may then intervene to restrict or eliminate the taxing rights originating from domestic law where a person, usually but not necessarily the taxpayer identified under domestic law, is eligible for the benefits of the tax convention in relation to that income.

28. The clear rule of Article 1 of the Model Tax Convention is that only persons who are residents of the Contracting States are entitled to the benefits of the tax Convention entered into by these States. Where income is earned by a partnership, the issue of whether the partnership itself is entitled to the benefits of the Convention will depend on whether the partnership qualifies as a person who is a resident of a Contracting State under the definitions of Article 3 and of paragraph 1 of Article 4.

a) Is a partnership a "person"?

29. For a partnership, entitlement to treaty benefits will therefore first depend on whether it qualifies as a "person". Subparagraph 1 *a)* of Article 3 of the Model defines a "person" for purposes of the Convention as "an individual, a company and any other body of persons". Paragraph 2 of the Commentary on Article 3 provides:

> "The definition of the term "person" given in subparagraph *a)* is not exhaustive and should be read as indicating that the term "person" is used in a very wide sense (cf. especially Articles 1 and 4). The definition explicitly mentions individuals, companies and other bodies of persons. From the meaning assigned to the term "company" by the definition contained in subparagraph *b)* it follows that, in addition, the term "person" includes any entity which, although itself not a body of persons, is treated as a body corporate for tax purposes. Thus, e.g. a foundation (*fondation, Stiftung*) may fall within the meaning of the term "person". Special considerations for the application of the Convention to partnerships are found in paragraphs 2 to 6 of the Commentary on Article 1."

30. The Commentary on Article 1, however, does not discuss the issue of whether a partnership is a "person" within the meaning of Article 3. While the practices of Member countries are not entirely uniform in this respect, the Committee has determined that partnerships should be considered to be "persons" within the meaning of the definition found in Article 3. In most countries, partnerships (as well as the individual partners) will be considered to be "persons" within the meaning of Article 3 either because the partnerships fall within the definition of company or because they are bodies of persons.

APPLICATION OF THE MODEL TAX CONVENTION TO PARTNERSHIPS

The Committee has therefore decided to delete the last sentence of paragraph 2 of the Commentary on Article 3 and to replace it with the following sentence:

> "Partnerships will also be considered to be "persons" either because they fall within the definition of "company" or, where this is not the case, because they constitute other bodies of persons."

31. The Committee has noted, however, that the definition of the term "national" in subdivision 1 *f)* (*ii*) of Article 3 may give rise to an implication that partnerships are not "persons" for purposes of the Convention. That definition provides that the term "national" includes "any legal person, partnership or association deriving its status as such from the laws in force in a Contracting State". As a matter of grammar and logic, a specific term that is included within a broader general term is not ordinarily given separate mention in a list that contains the general term.[1]

32. In order to avoid any confusion that may result from that definition, the Committee has agreed to add the following paragraph to the Commentary on Article 3:

> "The separate mention of partnerships in sub-paragraph 1 *f)* is not inconsistent with the status of a partnership as a person under sub-paragraph 1 *a)*. Under the domestic laws of some countries, it is possible for an entity to be a "person" but not a "legal person" for tax purposes. The explicit statement is necessary to avoid confusion."

b)   Is a partnership a "resident of a Contracting State"?

33. Paragraph 3 of the Commentary on Article 1 deals specifically with the problem of whether a partnership qualifies as a "resident" for treaty purposes. The Commentary states:

> "First, the question arises whether a partnership as such may invoke the provisions of the Convention. Where a partnership is treated as a company or taxed in the same way, it may reasonably be argued that the partnership is a resident of the Contracting State taxing the partnership on the grounds mentioned in paragraph 1

---

1.   Since partnerships qualify as "persons", they should be entitled, under paragraph 1 of Article 25, to have recourse to the mutual agreement procedure. Where, however, a partnership does not qualify as a "resident of a Contracting State" (see below), paragraph 1 of Article 25 does not indicate to which competent authority it should present its case. The Committee believes that this procedural hurdle should not prevent the partnership from presenting its case to the competent authority of the State of residence of its partners since the same result could be obtained, albeit in a more cumbersome way, if each of the partners presented the case himself.

of Article 4 and therefore, falling under the scope of the Convention, is entitled to the benefits of the Convention. In the other instances mentioned in paragraph 2 above, the application of the Convention to the partnership as such might be refused, at least if no special rule is provided for in the Convention covering partnerships."

34. The Committee discussed this paragraph and concluded that its analysis is correct. If the State in which a partnership has been organised treats that partnership as fiscally transparent, then the partnership is not "liable to tax" in that State within the meaning of Article 4, and so cannot be a resident for purposes of the Convention. Although inconvenient at times (e.g. paragraph 89 below), there appears to be little scope for a contrary argument under the current wording of Article 4.

35. To clarify this point, the Committee has agreed to delete the last sentence of paragraph 3 of the Commentary on Article 1 and to replace it with the following sentences:

"Where, however, a partnership is treated as fiscally transparent in a State, the partnership is not "liable to tax" in that State within the meaning of paragraph 1 of Article 4, and so cannot be a resident thereof for purposes of the Convention. In such a case, the application of the Convention to the partnership as such would be refused, unless a special rule covering partnerships were provided for in the Convention. Where the application of the Convention is so refused, the partners are entitled, with respect to their share of the income of the partnership, to the benefits provided by the Conventions entered into by the States of which they are residents to the extent that the partnership's income is allocated to them for the purposes of taxation in their State of residence (cf. paragraph 8.2 of the Commentary on Article 4)."

36. The Committee recognised that the determination of whether a partnership is "liable to tax" in a given State may present practical difficulties having regard to the different systems that countries use to impose tax on partnerships' income. It believes that the list referred to in paragraph 22 above, which is included in Annex III, would assist countries in dealing with these difficulties.

37. The Committee discussed in detail how the concept of "liable to tax" should be understood in the context of different systems for taxing partnerships' income. The Committee first discussed cases where domestic tax laws create intermediary situations where a partnership is partly treated as a taxable unit and partly disregarded for tax purposes. While this may create practical difficulties with respect to a very limited number of partnerships, it is a more important problem in the case of other entities such as trusts. For this reason, the Committee decided to deal with this issue in the context of follow-up work to this report.

APPLICATION OF THE MODEL TAX CONVENTION TO PARTNERSHIPS

38. The Committee then examined two common approaches to taxation of partnerships. In many countries, the tax laws provide that income derived by a partnership from a particular source must be computed at the partnership level as if the partnership were a distinct taxpayer. Each partner is then allocated his share of that income which retains its character and is added to his income for purposes of determining his taxable income. His taxable income, including his share of the partnership's income is then reduced by the personal allowances and deductions to which he is entitled and tax is then determined, assessed and paid at the partner's level. In such cases, it is clear that the partnership is not itself liable to tax.

39. In other countries, the income and the tax payable is computed in a similar way, but the tax payable by the partners is then aggregated at the level of the partnership which is then assessed for the total amount of the tax. In these cases, the assessment of the tax in the hands of the partnership is a collection technique that does not change the fact that the tax payable on the income of the partnership is determined at each partner's level taking into account the other income of that partner, the personal allowances to which he is entitled and the tax rate applicable to him (which may vary depending on his total income or his nature). In such cases, the partnership is also not liable to tax.

40. The Committee agreed that for purposes of determining whether a partnership is liable to tax, the real question is whether the amount of tax payable on the partnership income is determined in relation to the personal characteristics of the partners (whether the partners are taxable or not, what other income they have, what are the personal allowances to which they are entitled and what is the tax rate applicable to them). If the answer to that question is yes, then the partnership should not itself be considered to be liable to tax. The fact that the income is computed at the level of the partnership before being allocated to the partners, that the tax is technically paid by the partnership or that it is assessed on the partnership as described in the preceding paragraph will not change that result.

41. The fact that a partnership may be said to be liable to tax in a State will not, however, be sufficient for it to be considered a resident of that State for purposes of tax conventions. Paragraph 1 of Article 4 also requires that the liability to tax in that State be caused by one of the criteria listed therein (e.g. residence, domicile etc.). Thus, for a partnership to be a resident of a Contracting State, it has to be liable to tax in that State by reason of one of these criteria.

42. The provisions of tax conventions will apply differently depending on whether or not a partnership qualifies as a resident. Where a partnership does not so qualify because it is the partners who are liable to tax on the partnership's income, the income derived by the partnership should be considered to keep the nature and source that it had in the hands of the partnership for purposes of the provisions of a tax convention. This corresponds to the situation that is generally provided for under the domestic laws of the countries that

do not treat partnerships as taxable entities. Thus, where a partnership is treated as transparent for purposes of tax conventions because it is the partners rather than the partnerships who are liable to tax on the partnership's income, that income will, when applying the relevant Convention, keep the nature and source that it had in the hands of the partnership for purposes of taxation in the hands of the partners.[1]

43. While the Convention generally does not apply to partnerships that are treated as fiscally transparent since they do not meet the criteria of paragraph 1 of Article 4, some countries have included partnerships within the coverage of their Conventions in certain circumstances. In specially negotiated provisions, the partnership is treated as a resident to the extent that its income is subject to tax in the hands of the partners. This can come about because the partners are resident in the State in which the partnership is organised or because, in the case of non-resident partners, the partnership maintains a permanent establishment in the State of organisation and the income is attributable to the permanent establishment. If all of the income of the partnership is attributed to either resident partners or to a permanent establishment when non-resident partners are present, the partnership would be treated in the same way as a resident company which was subject to worldwide tax liability. The following text from the Protocol to the Convention between Germany and Italy illustrates the use of such specially negotiated provisions:

> "A partnership is deemed to be a resident of a Contracting State in the sense of paragraph 1 of Article 4 if it has been established in accordance with the law of that State or if the main object of its activities is in that State. However, the limitations to the right to tax of the other Contracting State as provided in Articles 6 to 23 apply only insofar as the income derived from that State or the capital situated therein is subject to tax in the first-mentioned State.

44. One justification for such special provisions treating the partnership itself as resident is that they are viewed by some countries as avoiding the administrative problems involved in requiring that all partners establish that they are entitled to treaty benefits. In addition, in some cases, the provisions originated where one of the Contracting States treated partnerships as taxable entities and the other State, though applying a fiscal transparency approach, insisted on reciprocal treatment. Finally, since the income will necessarily be subject to tax in the State of organisation, providing treaty benefits will not result in double non-taxation or in the reduction of source State taxation where there is no tax in the State where the partnership has been formed.

45. On the other hand, there are some substantial problems and issues which such an approach raises. In the first place, it may be difficult to determine when the source State income is in fact attributable to a permanent establishment in the State of organisation. If

---

1. See the diverging opinion by France in Annex II.

APPLICATION OF THE MODEL TAX CONVENTION TO PARTNERSHIPS

the income was attributable to a third State's permanent establishment, for example, in a tax haven, the source State relief would not necessarily be matched with taxation in the State of organisation. Secondly, where the source State relief takes the form of a reduction in withholding tax, it is not clear how the reduction should be calculated where only a "part" of the partnership is treated as a treaty resident. The reduction might inure indirectly to the benefit of a partner not otherwise entitled to benefits. In addition, the existence of the partnership allows income which is attributed to a permanent establishment in the State of organisation to qualify for treaty benefits for a third State partner where the existence of a direct permanent establishment would not give rise to similar benefits.[1]

46. Given these difficulties, the Committee did not feel that the approach was promising enough to attempt to develop an alternative provision.

II.4 The partners' entitlement to treaty benefits when the partnership is not a resident

47. Where the partnership as such does not qualify as a resident under the principles developed in the preceding section, the Committee agrees that the partners should be entitled to the benefits provided by the Conventions entered into by the countries of which they are residents to the extent that they are liable to tax on their share of the partnership income in those countries. The following introductory examples illustrate the results which the Committee believes are appropriate in some commonly recurring situations. It is important to note that the solutions developed in this report do not exclude the possibility that Member countries may in their bilateral relations develop different solutions to the problems of double taxation which may arise in connection with partnerships.

---

1. See the diverging opinion by Germany in Annex II.

Example 1: *P is a partnership established in State P. A and B are P's partners who reside in State P. Both States P and S treat P as a transparent entity. P derives interest income from State S that is not attributable to a permanent establishment in State S.*

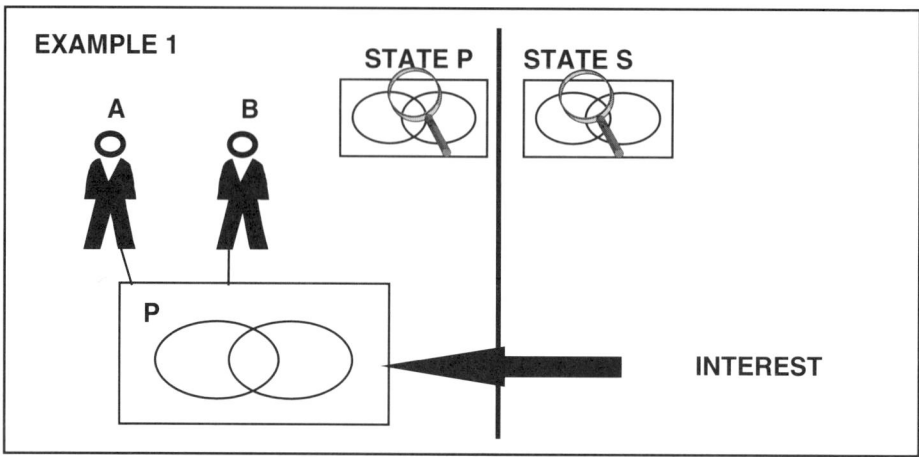

48. In this example, State S would likely determine that, under its domestic law, the relevant taxpayers are A and B. After applying its domestic law, it would then consider the application of the S-P tax Convention and, in particular, Article 11. Under paragraph 1 of Article 11, the Article applies to interest that is "paid to a resident of another state." In these circumstances, the income is appropriately viewed as "paid" to A and B since it is to them and not to the partnership that the income is allocated for purposes of determining their tax liability in State P. They thus have derived the income in the sense which is relevant for the application of the treaty. In effect, the source State should view the income as having "flowed through" the transparent partnership to the partners who are liable to tax on that income in the state of their residence.

APPLICATION OF THE MODEL TAX CONVENTION TO PARTNERSHIPS

Example 2: *P is an entity established in State P. A and B are P's partners who reside in State R. States R, P and S all treat P as a transparent entity. P derives interest income from State S that is not attributable to a permanent establishment in State S.*

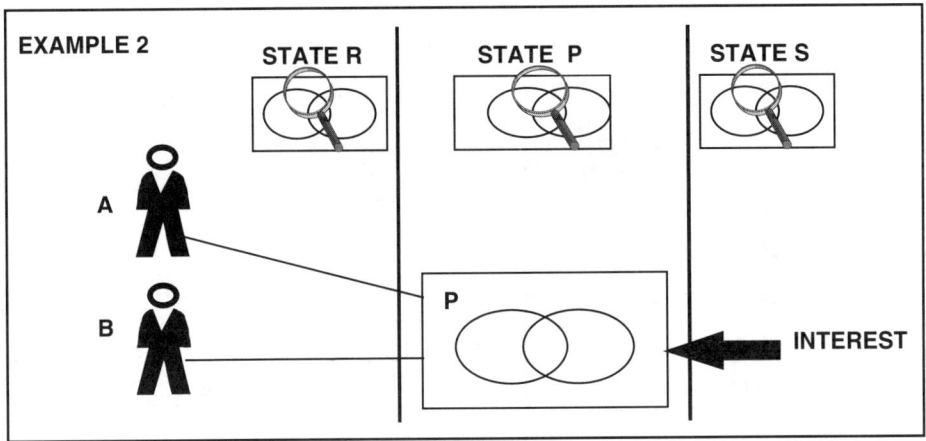

49. This example extends the basic principle illustrated in example 1 to a more complex situation involving three countries and two Conventions. As regards State S, again it will begin the analysis by determining that under its domestic law, the relevant taxpayers are A and B. In applying the S-R treaty, it would likewise determine that A and B have been allocated the income by State R and thus are liable to tax on that income for purposes of determining their entitlement to benefits under the Convention. By contrast, P may not claim benefits under the S-P Convention since it is not a resident of State P (it is not liable to tax in that State).

50. Such cases, in which the partners are not residents in the State where the partnership has been organised, raise additional difficulties for tax authorities wishing to verify a taxpayer's entitlement to treaty benefits. Clearly, states should not be expected to grant the benefits of tax conventions in cases where they cannot verify whether a person is truly entitled to these benefits. Thus, the application of the provisions of the S-R Convention will be conditional on State S being able to obtain all the necessary information.

Example 3: *P is an entity established in State P. A and B are P's partners who reside in State R. States P and S both treat P as a transparent entity but State R treats it as taxable entity. P derives business profits from State S that is not attributable to a permanent establishment in State S.*

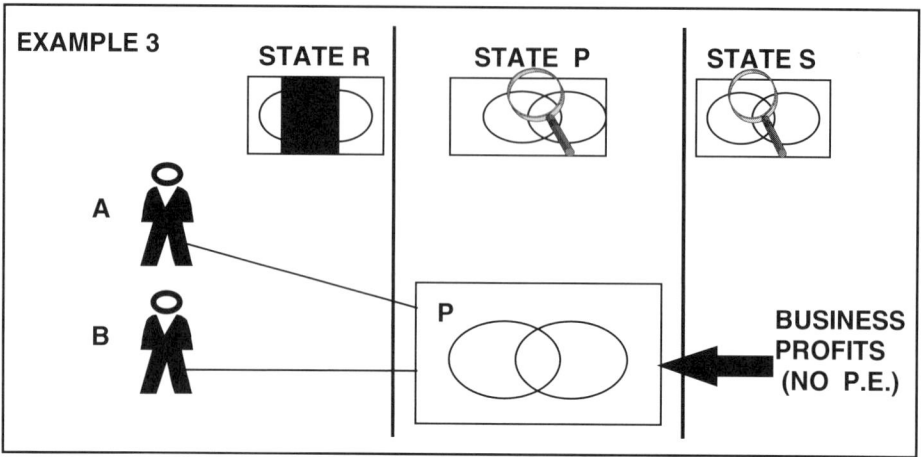

51. Here, unlike the first two examples, there is a difference in the allocation of the income involved among the countries. State S under its domestic law treats A and B as the relevant taxpayers. However, when it comes to apply the S-R treaty, it is crucial that State R, while it generally treats A and B as residents, does not allocate to them the income arising in State S since, under the domestic law of State R, that income is allocated to P, an entity which is not resident, i.e. not liable to tax in State R. Thus in these circumstances, State S would not be required to extend the benefits of the Convention to the income which State R allocates to P for purposes of determining the liability to State R's tax on that income, a conclusion which may be reached by a number of different routes as explained below. Correspondingly, for purposes of applying the S-R Convention, the treatment of P in State P is not relevant, though of course it would be important in the application of the S-P Convention as will be discussed in subsequent examples.

52. The Committee views the outcome in the above examples as resulting from an application of the Convention that takes account of the basic purposes of the Convention: to eliminate double taxation and to prevent double non-taxation. As discussed in the introductory section of this report, it recognises that the existing Convention and its Commentary do not deal explicitly with many of the issues which arise in the treatment of partnerships under the Convention. Under a literal application of the provisions of the Convention, a partnership that is not itself liable to tax would not be entitled to the

benefits of the Convention and to the extent that the income derived by or paid to the partnership would not be considered to be derived by or paid to the partners themselves, the partners would also be precluded from claiming the benefits of the Convention with respect to the partnership's income. To avoid the result that the provisions of tax conventions do not apply to the income of a transparent partnership, it is therefore necessary to determine whether and how it would be possible to obtain the desired results under the structure of the existing Convention.

53. One broadly based approach would be to recognise as implicit in the structure of the Convention the principle that the source State, in applying the Convention where partnerships are involved, should take into account, as part of the factual context in which the Convention is to be applied, the way in which an item of income arising in its jurisdiction is treated in the jurisdiction of the taxpayer claiming the benefits of the treaty as a resident. If that State "flows through" the income to the partner, then the partner should be considered liable to tax and entitled to the benefits of the Convention of the State of which he is a resident. It may be observed, in that respect, that a partner is still to be considered liable to tax on the income which "flows through" to him where, in the State of residence, tax is not imposed on that income by virtue of, e.g. a participation exemption in the case of dividends or the application of the exemption method for the relief of double taxation in the case of income attributable to a permanent establishment. On the other hand, if the income, though allocated to the taxpayer under the laws of the source State, is not similarly allocated for purposes of determining the liability to tax on that item of income in the State of residence of the taxpayer claiming the benefits of the Convention, then the source State should not grant benefits under the Convention. In these latter circumstances, the underlying factual premise on which the allocation of taxing rights is based, that is, that the source State is only obliged to reduce its domestic law tax claim where the income in question is potentially liable to tax in the hands of a resident of the treaty partner, is simply not present. This interpretation, which looks at how the partnership's income is taxed by the State of residence, avoids denying the benefits of tax conventions to a partnership's income on the basis that neither the partnership, because it is not a resident, nor the partners, because the income is not directly paid to them or derived by them, can claim the benefits of the Convention with respect to that income.

54. Another approach would involve consideration of the terms of the distributive rules in the relevant Articles of the Convention. Under that analysis, in the case of dividends, interest and royalties, the inquiry would be whether or not the recipient of the item of income was the beneficial owner of the income under the laws of the State of residence of the taxpayer claiming treaty benefits and thus the taxpayer in relation to the income. In the case of a partnership treated as transparent under the laws of the source State but as a taxable entity under the laws of the residence State, the entity itself and not the partners would be treated as the beneficial owner. Because of the treatment of the income in the State of residence, the partners would not be the beneficial owners of the

income for purposes of the treaty. Thus the partners would not be entitled to treaty benefits in those circumstances and whether the entity was so entitled would depend on whether it independently qualified as a resident. Similarly, where business profits are involved, the determination of whether the profits were attributable to an enterprise "of" the residence State of the taxpayer claiming the benefits would be determined by the source State on the basis of the treatment of the situation in the residence State. Again, if the partnership was treated as an entity by that latter State, it, and not the partners, would be the relevant party which would be required to establish a claim from treaty benefits.

55. Finally, some countries would feel constrained to follow the allocation of the income under their principles of domestic law, even when that results in the income being subject to taxation in the State of source and taxation in the hands of the partners under the law of their state of residence. Even those countries, however, recognise the desirability of some mechanism to relieve the resulting double taxation and either provide for the situation in special provisions in their Conventions or at least show a willingness to relieve the double taxation through the mechanism of the mutual agreement procedure, particularly where a distribution of partnership income is made in the year in which the income is realised.

56. In the light of the preceding analysis, the Committee has therefore agreed to add the following paragraph to the Commentary to Article 4:

> "8.2 Where a State disregards a partnership for tax purposes and treats it as fiscally transparent, taxing the partners on their share of the partnership income, the partnership itself is not liable to tax and may not, therefore, be considered to be a resident of that State. In such a case, since the income of the partnership "flows through" to the partners under the domestic law of that State, the partners are the persons who are liable to tax on that income and are thus the appropriate persons to claim the benefits of the Conventions concluded by the States of which they are residents. This latter result will obtain even if, under the domestic law of the State of source, the income is attributed to a partnership which is treated as a separate taxable entity. For States which could not agree with this interpretation of the Article, it would be possible to provide for this result in a special provision which would avoid the resulting potential double taxation where the income of the partnership is differently allocated by the two States."

57. The following examples examine some of the implications of this general approach, as outlined in paragraphs 52 and 53, and the results that it would generate in a variety of situations.

APPLICATION OF THE MODEL TAX CONVENTION TO PARTNERSHIPS

II.5 Entitlement to treaty benefits when one State treats the partnership as a taxable entity

58. The first set of situations involve cases where one of the States treats the partnership as a taxable entity and another State views it as fiscally transparent. This question is considered first in a bilateral setting then where triangular relations are present.

a) Bilateral cases

Example 4: *P is a partnership established in State P. A and B are P's partners who reside in State P. State P treats P as a transparent entity while State S treats it as a taxable entity. P derives royalty income from State S that is not attributable to a permanent establishment in State S.*

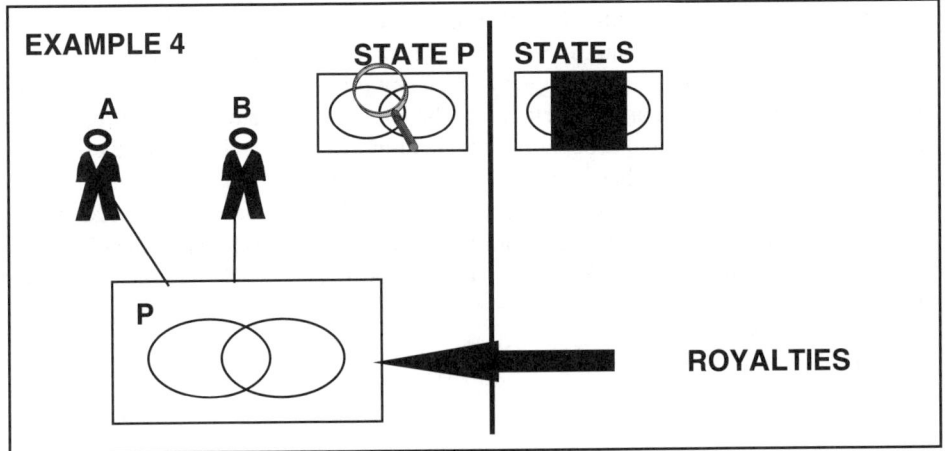

59. This example involves the fundamental difference in the tax treatment of partnerships that has already been referred to in paragraph 19 onwards above. The question is how the State S should apply the provisions of the Convention in such a case.

60. Under State S domestic law, the taxpayer will be partnership P. State S could then argue that since partnership P is not entitled to the benefits of the treaty, it can tax the income derived by P regardless of the provisions of the S-P Convention. This, however, would mean that the income on which A and B are liable to tax in State P would be subjected to tax in State S regardless of the Convention, a result that seems in direct conflict with the object and purpose of the Convention.

61. The Committee compared that approach, under which State S applies the provisions of the Convention by reference to the treatment of the partnership under its domestic law, with another approach, under which State S considers the entitlement to treaty benefits of A and B, both residents of State P, under the principles put forward above. Under the latter approach, State S would determine that the provisions of the Convention should be applied to prevent it from taxing the royalties since, under these principles, the income must be considered to be paid to A and B, two residents of State P, who should also be considered to be the beneficial owners of such income as these are the persons liable to tax on such income in State P. The Committee concluded that this approach was the correct one as it is more likely to ensure that the benefits of the Convention accrue to the persons who are liable to tax on the income.

62. The Committee did not consider this approach to be inconsistent with the provisions of paragraph 2 of Article 3, under which terms not defined in the Convention have, unless the context provides otherwise, the meaning which they have under the domestic law of the Contracting State that applies the Convention. In the example, the tax treatment of the partnership in State P is part of the facts on the basis of which the terms of the Convention are to be applied. Thus, by referring to that tax treatment, State S does not adopt a particular interpretation of the terms of the Convention put forward by State P; it merely takes into account of facts required for the application of these terms. The Committee concluded that, in any event, if an interpretation based on domestic law would lead to cases where the income taxed in the hands of residents of one State would not get the benefits of the Convention, a result that would be contrary to the object and purpose of the Convention, the context of the Convention would require a different interpretation.

APPLICATION OF THE MODEL TAX CONVENTION TO PARTNERSHIPS

Example 5: *The facts are the same as in example 4 but the tax treatment of the partnership in State P and S is reversed. P is a partnership established in State P. A and B are P's partners who reside in State P. State P treats P as a taxable entity while State S treats it as a transparent entity. P derives royalty income from State S that is not attributable to a permanent establishment in State S.*

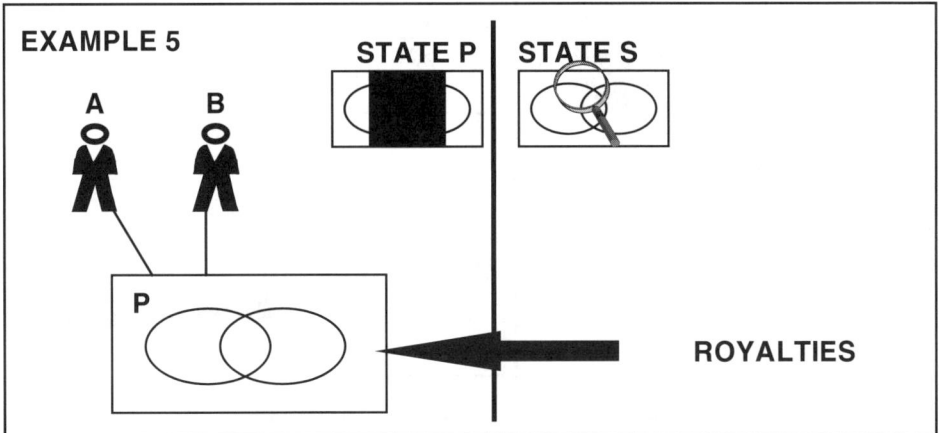

63. In this situation, in following its domestic law rules for allocating the income of the partnership, State S would treat A and B as the relevant taxpayers. However, in applying the treaty, the principles developed in subsection II.4 would require that it takes into consideration that State P had allocated the income of the partnership to P. Thus, for purposes of the Convention, P would be the taxpayer entitled to claim the benefits of the Convention since it is liable to tax in State P on the income of the partnership. While, in the particular circumstances of this example, it does not make a difference whether State S considers the treaty entitlements of the partners or of the partnership, this would matter, as shown in subsequent examples, if the partners, or one of them, were not residents of State P.

Example 6: *P is a partnership established in State P. A and B are P's partners who reside in State R. State P treats P as a transparent entity while State R treats it as a taxable entity. P derives royalty income from State P that is not attributable to a permanent establishment in that state.*

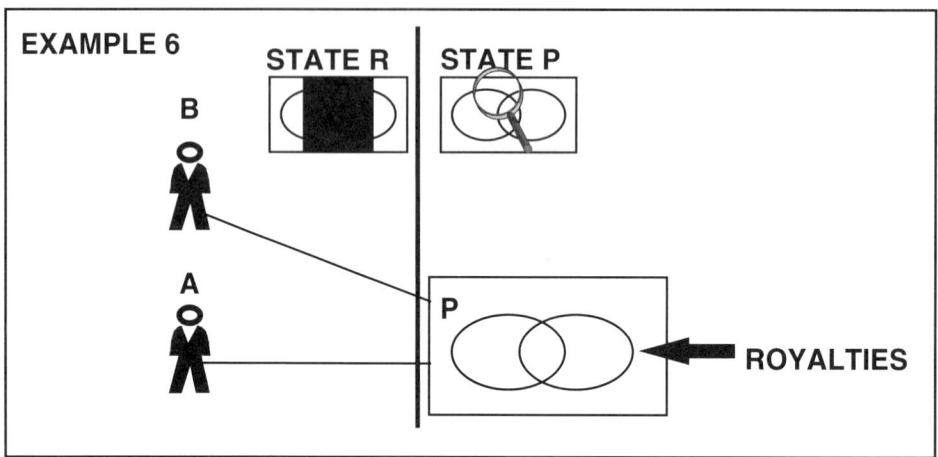

64. While the Committee agrees that in this situation State P should not be required to give the benefits of the Convention with respect to the royalty income, several different approaches are used to support this result. Using one approach, partners A and B, though residents as such of State R are not liable to tax on the partnership income under the allocation rules applied by State R, consequently they are not entitled to benefits under the Convention in respect of that income. P is not a resident of State R for purposes of the Convention since, from the perspective of State R, it is not a domestic taxpayer in any sense. Thus again, State P's right to tax the partnership income would not be restricted under the Convention.

65. Alternatively, as discussed in paragraph 54 above, the partners would not be entitled to benefits under the Convention because they would not be considered as beneficial owners of the income for purposes of the Convention. Adopting a more literal approach, State P might simply focus on the fact that, under its allocation rules, the income has been paid to P and P would not qualify as a resident either of State R or State P. Here the treatment of A and B would not be relevant.

66. Finally, some countries would deny treaty benefits to A and B based on concepts of bad faith or abuse of treaty rights. The distributive rules of the Convention are based on the underlying assumption that A and B would be attributed the income on which treaty relief would be granted and where that is not the case, these general concepts would allow State P to resist any claims by A or B for benefits.

APPLICATION OF THE MODEL TAX CONVENTION TO PARTNERSHIPS

67. Example 18 below deals with the tax treatment of the subsequent distribution by P of the partnership profits to A and B.

b)   Triangular cases

68. Triangular cases pose difficult problems with respect to the determination of the entitlement to treaty benefits. The Committee believes, however, that these problems may be solved through the application of the same principles put forward in paragraphs 52 and 53 above. The following examples discuss how these principles should be applied in different situations involving three states.

Example 7: *P is a partnership established in State P. A and B are P's partners who reside in State R. P owns shares in X, a company that is a resident of State S. X pays a dividend to P. States R and S treat P as a taxable entity while State P treats it as fiscally transparent.*

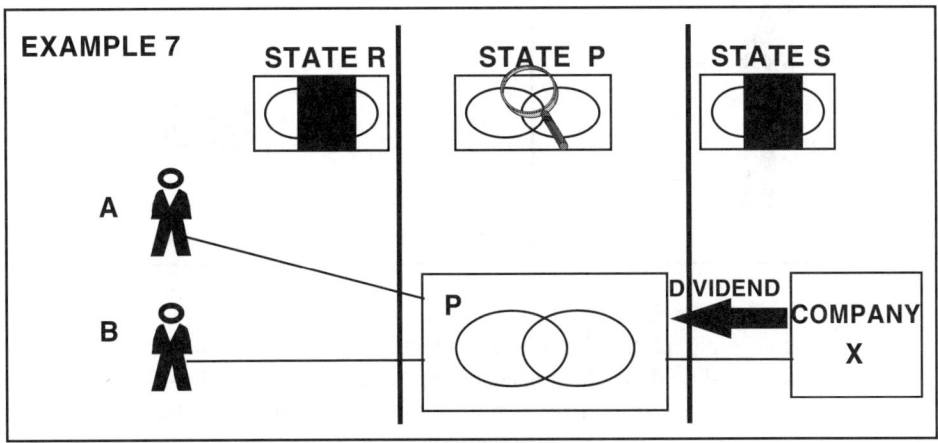

69. In this situation, the partnership is not liable to tax in State P and is therefore not a resident of that state for purposes of the P-S Convention. Similarly, though P is treated as the taxpayer for purposes of the domestic law of State S and the income is allocated to P under the domestic laws of R, P is not liable to tax in State R because it is not treated as a resident. Finally, though A and B are potentially liable to tax as residents in State R, under R's allocation rules, the income is not allocated to them but to P. Thus P is not a resident of State R and A and B are not entitled to benefit from the R-S Convention with respect to the partnership's income. State S would thus be entitled to tax the income without restriction.

70. It should be noted that, in this example (as in the following examples), the tax treatment of partnerships in State S does not have any impact on the entitlement to treaty benefits. Thus, the S-R and S-P Conventions would still not be applicable with respect to the dividends if State S treated partnerships as transparent rather than taxable entities.

Example 8: *The facts are the same as in example 7 except that the tax treatment of the partnership in State P is reversed. P is a partnership established in State P. A and B are P's partners who reside in State R. P owns shares in X, a company that is a resident of State S. X pays a dividend to P. All States treat P as a taxable entity.*

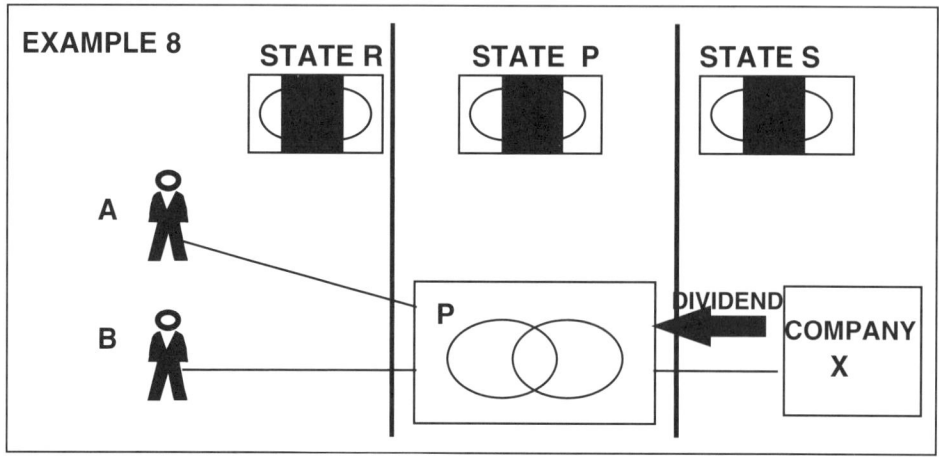

71. In this example, partnership P is a resident of State P as it is liable to tax therein. Partners A and B should not be considered to be entitled to the benefits of the S-R Convention with respect to the partnership income as they are not liable to tax on that income. Conversely, P should be considered by State S to be entitled to the benefits of the S-P Convention in relation with the dividends it derives from that State as it is liable to tax on those dividends and should therefore be considered to be the recipient and beneficial owner of that income. Thus the S-P Convention will restrict State S right to tax the dividends, even if State S taxes the dividends in the hands of partners A and B under its domestic rules applicable to the taxation of partnerships. It should be noted, however, that since P is a partnership, it will not get the benefits of the reduced rate of tax provided for in subparagraph 2a) of Article 10 of the Model Tax Convention (the subparagraph expressly excludes partnerships from its application) unless the two Contracting States agree to modify subparagraph 2a) to give the benefits of the reduced rate to a partnership treated as a body corporate (cf. paragraph 11 of the Commentary on Article 10).

APPLICATION OF THE MODEL TAX CONVENTION TO PARTNERSHIPS

72.   As already mentioned, the tax treatment of partnerships in State S does not have any impact on the entitlement to treaty benefits in this case. Thus, the S-P Convention would still be the only relevant one if State S treated partnerships as transparent rather than taxable entities.

Example 9: *The facts are the same as in example 8 except that the tax treatment of the partnership in State R is reversed. P is a partnership established in State P. A and B are P's partners who reside in State R. P owns shares in X, a company that is a resident of State S. X pays a dividend to P. State P and State S treat P as a taxable entity while State R treats it as fiscally transparent.*

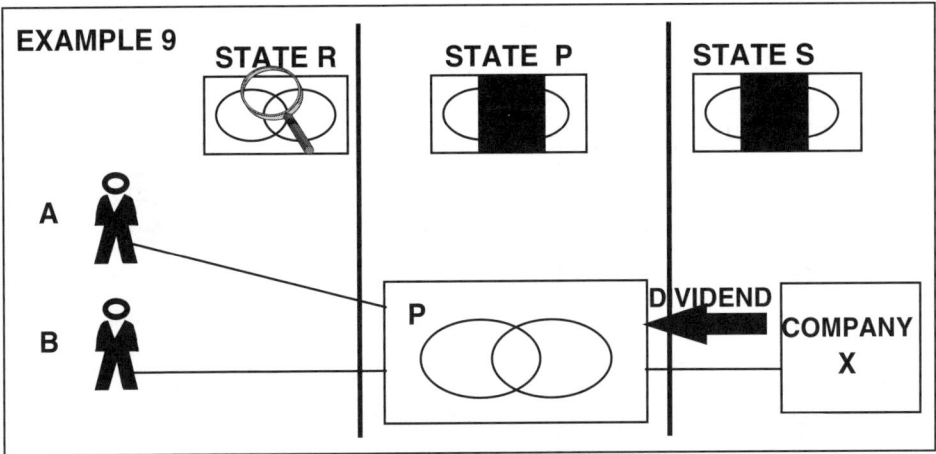

73.   This example presents a case where there will be a double entitlement to treaty benefits with respect to the same income. As in the previous example, partnership P is a resident of State P as it is liable to tax therein. P should again be considered by State S to be entitled to the benefits of the S-P Convention in relation with the dividends it derives from that State as it is liable to tax on those dividends and should therefore be considered to be the recipient and beneficial owner of that income. In contrast to the previous example, however, partners A and B should also be considered to be entitled to the benefits of the S-R Convention with respect to the partnership income as they are also liable to tax on that income. Thus both the S-P and S-R Conventions will restrict State S right to tax the dividends, regardless of whether State S taxes these dividends in the hands of the partnership or of partners A and B (under its domestic rules applicable to the taxation of partnerships, it will likely tax them in the hands of the partnership). Again, the tax treatment of partnerships in State S will not have any impact on this result so that both conventions would still be applicable if State S treated partnerships as transparent rather than taxable entities.

ISSUES IN INTERNATIONAL TAXATION

74. The Committee agreed that this double entitlement to treaty benefits will be satisfied by State S imposing the lowest amount of tax allowed under the two treaties. Thus, if the S-R Convention restricts to 15% of the gross amount of the dividends the tax that can be levied by State S while the S-P treaty restricts the tax to 10% of that amount, the obligations imposed on State S under both conventions will be satisfied if the tax imposed by State S does not exceed 10% of the dividends.

75. While the Committee agreed on that approach, it recognized the administrative difficulties that its implementation would generate in the case of a partnership that would have a large number of partners who would be residents of different States.

Example 10: *The facts are the same as in example 9 except that there is no tax convention between States S and P.*

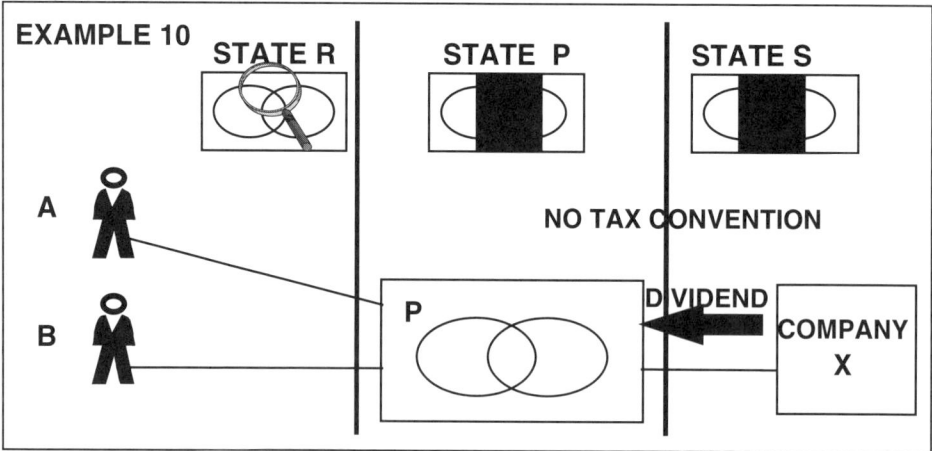

76. The Committee also discussed how the principles and conclusions formulated in its analysis of the previous examples would apply if the partnership were a resident of a state with which the State of source did not have a tax convention, including the case where the partnership was a resident of a tax haven. It concluded that same conclusions should apply as concerns the application of the Convention between the State of source and the State of residence of the partners.

77. Thus, in this example, partners A and B should be considered to be entitled to the benefits of the S-R Convention in respect of the dividends as they are both taxable in State R on these dividends.

78. As already noted, States should not, however, be expected to grant the benefits of a tax convention in cases where they cannot verify whether a person is truly entitled to these benefits. Thus if State P is a tax haven from which State S cannot obtain tax information, the application of the provisions of the S-R Convention will be conditional on State S being able to obtain all the necessary information from the partners or from State R. In such cases, State S might well decide to use the refund mechanism for the purposes of applying the limitation of tax provided for in Article 10 even though it normally applies this limitation at the time of the payment.

II.6 Application of the Convention where the benefits are dependent upon certain characteristics or attributes of the taxpayer

79. As indicated in paragraph 21 above, differences in how States apply the transparency approach may create difficulties for the application of tax conventions. Where a State considers that a partnership does not qualify as a resident because it is not liable to tax and the partners are liable to tax in their State of residence on their share of the partnership's income, it is expected that that State will apply the provisions of the Convention as if the partners had earned the income directly so that the classification of the income for purposes of the allocative rules of Articles 6 to 21 will not be modified by the fact that the income flows-through the partnership.

80. Difficulties may arise, however, in the application of provisions which refer to the activities of the taxpayer, the nature of the taxpayer, the relationship between the taxpayer and another party to a transaction. States may have different views as to what extent the partnership should be ignored in applying such rules. The following subsections describe how the Committee believes that some of the provisions of the Convention should be applied in that respect.

a)   Construction activities

Example 11: *Company A carries on a business of engineering and company B carries on a business of electrical installation. Both companies are residents of State P. They have established a partnership P in State P for the purpose of a contract to design and install the electrical equipment in a nuclear reactor being built in State S. As part of the obligations of P under the contract, employees of Company A will be present on the construction site from 1 January to June 10 and employees of Company B will be there from 10 June to 1 February. When performing their duties, these employees will act as employees of the respective companies, each company acting as agent for the partnership.*

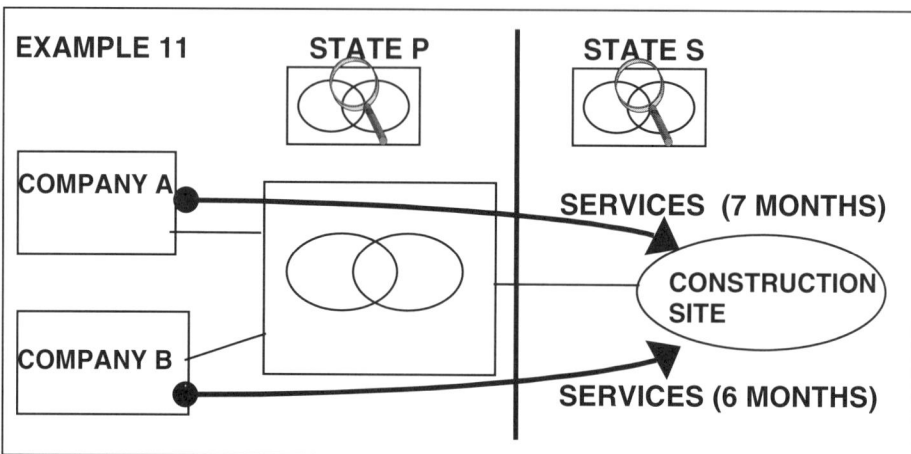

81.   In this example, the Committee concluded that the period of time spent by the two partners should be aggregated at the partnership level with the result that the 12 month limit of paragraph 3 of Article 5 is exceeded. The enterprise carried on by the partnership will therefore be considered to have a permanent establishment in State S so that each partner will be considered to have a permanent establishment in State S for purposes of the taxation of their share of the business profits derived by the partnership from State S. This conclusion would not hold good if the relationship between A and B constituted merely a joint venture or consortium rather than a partnership.

APPLICATION OF THE MODEL TAX CONVENTION TO PARTNERSHIPS

b) Income attributable to the fixed base of a partnership

Example 12: *Partnership P, which has been established in State P, has a fixed base in State R. Partner A is a resident of State P and partner B is a resident of State R. They have agreed to divide the profits of the partnership equally. P earns 1,500,000 during the taxable period. 1,000,000 of that amount is attributable to the services performed by B from the State R fixed base. The remaining 500,000 is attributable to services performed by A in State P. Both States treat partnerships as transparent entities.*

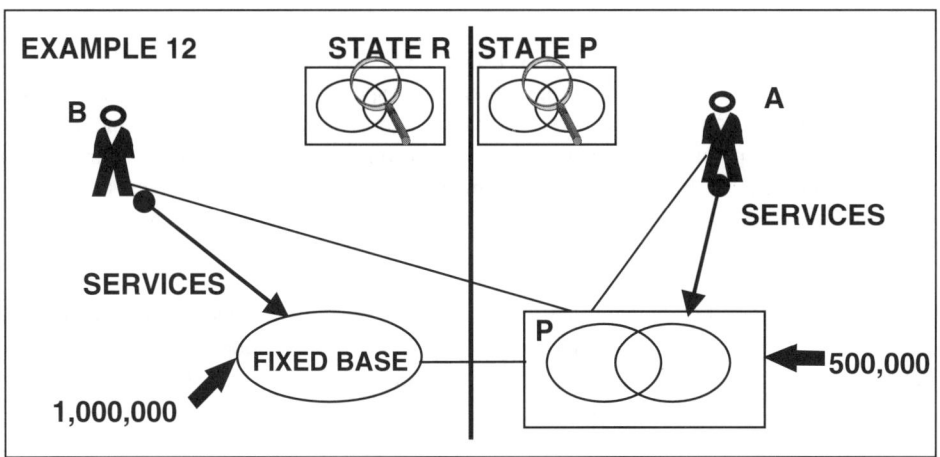

82. This example raises the question of the extent to which a transparent partnership should be ignored for purposes of the application of Articles 7 and 14. The Committee agreed that under Article 14, P's fixed base in State R should be considered to be a fixed base of both A and B and that the same is true for a permanent establishment under Article 7.

83. The Committee then considered to what extent the activities of the partnership could be similarly allocated to each of the partners for the purposes of applying paragraph 1 of Article 14, which require that the fixed base be regularly available to a person "for the purpose of performing his activities".

84. Two views were expressed. Under the first view, the reference to "his activities" in paragraph 1 of Article 14 refer to the personal activities of each partner and the partnership's activities cannot be flowed-through to the partners. According to that view, Article 14 would not allow State R to tax partner A on his share of the income attributable to the fixed base (500,000) since the fixed base was not regularly available to A for the purposes of his own personal activities.

85. The majority, however, agreed with the different view that the activities of the partnership should be allocated to the partners to the same extent that the fixed base of the partnership is attributed to each of them. Applying this approach to the above example, State R would be allowed, as a source State, to tax partners A and partner B on their respective share of the income attributable to the fixed base located therein. State R will also be allowed, as the residence State, to tax partner B's share of any other partnership income. Similarly, State P will be allowed, as a source State, to tax all the partnership's income attributable to the fixed base of the partnership that is located in that State.

86. The Committee realised, however, that cases in the real world are rarely as simple as this example. The partnership agreement may specifically allocate the income from various States to particular partners. Entities that may be considered as partnerships for some purposes may not be partnerships for tax purposes; many international partnerships grant considerable autonomy, both managerial and financial, to their in-country subsidiary organisations. Both taxpayers and tax authorities strive to avoid administratively unmanageable results.

87. The Committee decided that these issues would more appropriately be dealt with in the context of its work on issues related to Article 14. It noted, however, that there should not be differences in result whether Article 7 or 14 applied and that a different conclusion would give rise to difficulties.

c) *Determination of "employer" for purposes of Article 15*

88. During its discussion of whether partnerships qualify as residents for purposes of tax conventions, the Committee also examined a related issue arising from the reference to the concept of resident in subparagraph 2*b*) of Article 15. Paragraph 2 of Article 15 exempts employment income earned by a resident of a Contracting State in the other State from tax by that other State if a number of conditions apply. One such condition is that the employer must not be a resident of the state in which the employment income is earned. The application of this rule may be problematic when the employer is a partnership.

89. As discussed above, a partnership that is treated as a transparent entity by a Contracting State does not qualify as a resident of that State under Article 4. While it is clear that a partnership that is treated as a transparent entity could qualify as an "employer" (especially under the domestic law definitions of the term in some countries, e.g. where an employer is defined as a person liable for a wage tax), the application of the condition imposed by subparagraph 2*b*) of Article 15 at the level of the partnership regardless of the situation of the partners would render the condition totally meaningless because the partnership cannot possibly qualify as a resident by virtue of its transparent status.

90. The Committee examined this result in the context of Article 15 and in light of the object and purpose of subparagraphs *2b)* and *c)* of that Article. In its view, the conditions imposed by these subparagraphs aim at avoiding the source taxation of short-term employments to the extent that the employment income is not allowed as a deductible expense in the State of source because the employer is not taxable in that State since he is not resident nor has a permanent establishment therein. These subparagraphs can also be justified by the fact that imposing source deduction requirements with respect to short-term employments in a given State may be considered to be constitute an excessive administrative burden where the employer neither resides nor has a permanent establishment in that State.[1]

91. On that basis, the Committee concluded that in order to achieve a meaningful interpretation that would accord with the context and the object of paragraph 2 of Article 15, subparagraph 2b) should, in the case of partnerships treated as transparent entities, be considered to refer to the partners of such a partnership. Thus, the Committee favours an interpretation where the concepts of "employer" and "resident", as found in subparagraph *2b)*, are applied at the level of the partners rather than at the level of the partnership. This approach is fully consistent with that put forward in paragraphs 81 and 85 above, under which certain provisions of tax conventions must be applied at the partners' level rather than at that of the partnership in order to avoid absurd or unreasonable results.

92. The Committee realised that this interpretation would create difficulties where the partners resided in different States. Such difficulties, however, could be addressed through the mutual agreement procedure by reference, for example, to the State in which the partners who own the majority of the interests in the partnership reside (i.e. the State in which the greatest part of the deduction will be claimed).

III. APPLICATION OF TAX CONVENTIONS BY THE STATE OF RESIDENCE

93. Where partnerships are involved, the application of tax conventions by the State of residence also raise difficulties, primarily with respect to the application of Article 23 on Elimination of Double Taxation. This Chapter examines some of these difficulties. Section III.1 focuses on the particular problem of conflicts of qualification while section III.2 focuses on other problems that conflicts of income allocation may create for the State of residence.

---

1. See the diverging opinion by Germany in Annex II.

ISSUES IN INTERNATIONAL TAXATION

III.1   Conflicts of qualification

a)   Description of the problem

94.   The Committee has found that a number of difficulties relating to the application of tax conventions to partnerships fall in the broader category of so-called "conflicts of qualification", where the residence and source States apply different articles of the Convention on the basis of differences in their domestic law. Example 13 below illustrates such a conflict.

95.   Subsection b) presents the conclusions reached by the Committee. Subsection c) discusses various cases of conflicts of qualification involving partnerships on the basis of these conclusions, presenting the answer to example 13 in paragraph 119.

Example 13: *Partner A makes a loan to partnership P, which has been established in State P where it carries on a business through a permanent establishment. P pays interest to A. State P recognizes loans between partners and partnerships; under its domestic legislation State P allows P a tax deduction for the interest. State R does not recognize loans between partners and partnerships under its domestic law. Both States treat partnerships as transparent entities and apply Article 7 to the income of P, but State P applies Article 11 to the interest payment and State R does not.*

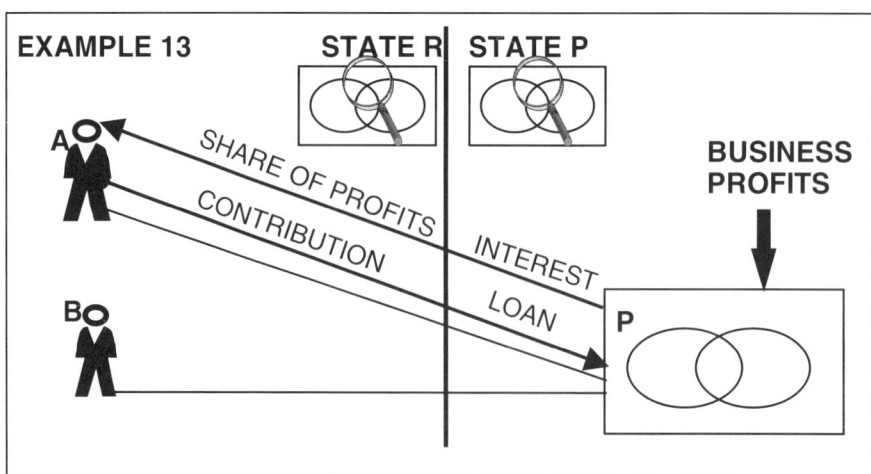

96.   In this example, while partner A is clearly entitled to the benefits of the R-P Convention, there is disagreement between States P and R as to which provisions of the Convention are applicable. State P, being the State of source of the income, applies its domestic laws for the purposes of taxing the income of and from the partnership. It

accordingly determines that partner A receives interest from the partnership and that Article 11 of the Convention applies to restrict to 10% the tax that it can impose on the interest. Under the domestic law of State R, there has been no loan and consequently A has no interest income. State R, however, will consider that the payment from P to A is a distribution of A's share of the business profits of the partnership which has been taxed upon realisation under Article 7.

97. The position of State P is in accordance with the provisions of the Convention. Pursuant to paragraph 2 of Article 3, State P has interpreted the word "debt-claims of every kind", which are found in paragraph 3 of Article 11, in accordance with its domestic law and has therefore concluded that a loan by a partner qualifies as a debt-claim on which interest may be paid. It has applied Article 11 of the Convention accordingly.

98. The consequences of the position taken by State P must, however, be examined in relation to the taxation of partner A in State R. One must distinguish, in that respect, the case where State R eliminates double taxation through the exemption method from that where it applies the credit method.

(i)   State R uses the exemption method

99. Under the domestic law of State R, there is no debt-claim between partner A and the partnership and A therefore does not derive interest from State P. If State R follows that position when considering its obligation to eliminate double taxation under Article 23A, that could lead it to consider that the payment made to partner A is a distribution of the partnership's business profits which is attributable to a permanent establishment situated in State P which constitutes income that must be exempted under paragraph 1 of Article 23A. To the extent that State P would have interpreted the Convention as obliging it to limit its tax to 10% of the gross amount of the payment, the result would be partial non-taxation (it would be total non-taxation if Article 11 of the R-P Convention did not provide for any source taxation of interest).

100. It must be noted that, regardless of the Convention, State R may still be obliged to exempt the income under its domestic tax rules related to the elimination of double taxation as these rules may require an other approach to be followed. This, however, would be a problem that could only be solved through an amendment to State R's domestic tax laws.

(ii) State R uses the credit method

101. Under the domestic law of State R, there is no debt-claim between partner A and the partnership and A therefore does not derive interest from State P. Even if State R follows that position when considering its obligation to eliminate double taxation under Article 23B, it should still tax any share of the partnership's income attributed to A so that non-taxation will be avoided.

b) *Analysis of the application of tax conventions in cases of conflicts of qualification*

102. The Committee agreed that, in addressing conflicts of qualification problems faced by the State of residence, a useful starting point is the recognition of the principle that the domestic law of the State applying its tax governs all matters regarding how and in the hands of whom an item of income is taxed. The effect of tax conventions can only be to limit or eliminate the taxing rights of the Contracting States. In the case of the source State, the right to tax items of income is limited by provisions based on Articles 6 through 21 of the Model Tax Convention. In the case of the residence State, while provisions based on Articles such as 8 and 19 might be relevant, the primary restriction would arise from the provisions of the Article on Elimination of Double Taxation (Article 23 in the Model Tax Convention), by which the residence State agrees to either exempt income that the source State may tax under the Convention or to give a credit for the tax levied by the source State on that item of income.

103. When taxing an item of income, the source State therefore applies its domestic law, subject to the restrictions and limitations imposed on it by the provisions of its tax conventions. The way that the State of residence qualifies an item of income for treaty purposes has no relevance on how and in the hands of whom the State of source taxes that item of income. The reverse, however, is not true. The way the State of residence eliminates double taxation will depend, to some extent, on how the Convention has been applied by the State of source.

104. The wording of Article 23 of the OECD Model Tax Convention is crucial in that respect. That article requires that relief be granted, either through the exemption or credit system, where an item of income may be taxed "in accordance with the provisions of the Convention". Thus, the State of residence has a treaty obligation to apply the exemption or credit method vis-à-vis any item of income where the tax convention authorizes taxation of that item of income by the State of source.

105. The meaning of the phrase "in accordance with the provisions of this Convention, may be taxed" needs to be clarified in that respect. Where, due to differences in the domestic law between the State of source and the State of residence, the former applies, with respect to a particular item of income, provisions of the Convention that are different from those that the State of residence would have applied to the same item of

income, the income is still being taxed in accordance with the provisions of the Convention, in this case as interpreted by the State of source. In such a case, therefore, Article 23 requires that relief from double taxation be granted by the State of residence notwithstanding the conflict of qualification resulting from these differences in domestic law.

106. It may be useful to consider the following example to examine the results of that approach.

Example 14: *Partner A, a resident of State R, sells his interest in P to D, a resident of State P, for an amount that exceeds A's adjusted basis in the interest. Under State R's domestic law, State R treats P as a company and would regard the gain as a capital gain of a resident of State R. Under State P's domestic law, State P treats P as fiscally transparent and would regard the gain as attributable to a State P permanent establishment.*

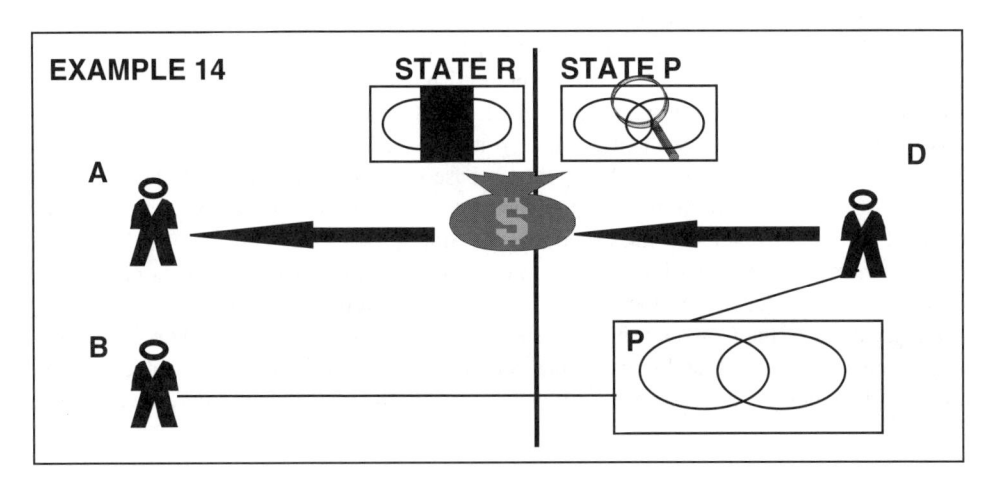

107. In this example, State P therefore considers that the alienation of the interest in the partnership is, for the purposes of its Convention with State R, an alienation by the partner of the underlying assets of the business carried on by the partnership, which may be taxed by State P according to paragraph 1 or 2 of Article 13. State R, as it treats the partnership as a corporate entity, considers that the alienation of the interest in the partnership is akin to the alienation of a share in a company, which could not be taxed by State P by reason of paragraph 4 of Article 13. In such a case, the conflict of qualification results exclusively from the different treatment of partnerships in the domestic laws of the two States and State P must be considered by State R to have taxed the gain from the alienation "in accordance with the provisions of the Convention" for purposes of the application of Article 23. State R must therefore grant an exemption or

give a credit pursuant to Article 23 of the Model Tax Convention irrespective of the fact that, under its own domestic law, it treats the alienation gain as income from the disposition of shares in a corporate entity and that, if State's P qualification of the income were consistent with that of State R, State R would not have to give relief under Article 23. No double taxation will therefore arise in such a case.

108. This does not mean that the wording of Article 23 requires the State of residence to eliminate double taxation in all cases where the State of source has imposed its tax by applying to an item of income a provision of the Convention that is different from that which the State of residence considers to be applicable. For instance, in the example above, if, for purposes of applying paragraph 2 of Article 13, State P considers that the partnership carried on business through a fixed place of business but State R argues that paragraph 4 applies because the partnership did not have a fixed place of business in State P, there is a legitimate dispute as to whether State P has taxed the income in accordance with the provisions of the Convention. The same may be said if State P, when applying paragraph 2 of Article 13, has interpreted the phrase "forming part of the business property" so as to include certain assets which would not fall within the meaning of that phrase according to the interpretation given to it by State R. Such conflicts resulting from different interpretation of facts or different interpretation of the provisions of the Convention must be distinguished from the conflicts of qualification described in the above paragraph where the divergence is based not on different interpretations of the provisions of the Convention, but on different provisions of domestic law. In the former case, the State of residence can argue that the State of source has not imposed its tax in accordance with the provisions of the Convention if it has applied its tax based on what the State of residence considers to be a wrong interpretation of the facts or a wrong interpretation of the Convention. States should use the provisions of Article 25 (Mutual Agreement Procedure), and in particular paragraph 3 thereof, in order to resolve this type of conflict when the difference in approaches would otherwise result in unrelieved double taxation.

109. In other situations, however, the phrase "in accordance with the provisions of this Convention, may be taxed" needs to be interpreted in relation to possible cases of double non-taxation involving residence States that follow the exemption method. Where the State of source considers that the provisions of the Convention preclude it from taxing an item of income which it would otherwise have taxed, the State of residence should, for purposes of applying paragraph 1 of Article 23A, consider that the item of income may not be taxed by the State of source in accordance with the provisions of the Convention, even though the State of residence would have applied the Convention differently so as to tax that income if it had been the State of source. Thus the State of residence is not required by paragraph 1 to exempt the item of income, a result which is consistent with the basic function of Article 23 which is to eliminate double taxation.

APPLICATION OF THE MODEL TAX CONVENTION TO PARTNERSHIPS

110. This situation may be illustrated by reference to the facts of the above example. A business is carried on through a fixed place of business in State P by a partnership established in that State and a partner, resident in State R, alienates his interest in that partnership. Changing the facts of the example, however, it is now assumed that State P treats the partnership as a taxable entity whereas State R treats it as fiscally transparent; it is further assumed that State R is an exemption State. State P, as it treats the partnership as a corporate entity, considers that the alienation of the interest in the partnership is akin to the alienation of a share in a company, which it cannot tax by reason of paragraph 4 of Article 13. State R, on the other hand, considers that the alienation of the interest in the partnership should have been taxable by State P as an alienation by the partner of the underlying assets of the business carried on by the partnership to which paragraph 1 or 2 of Article 13 would have been applicable. In determining whether it has the obligation to exempt the income under paragraph 1 of Article 23A, State R should nonetheless consider that, given the way that the provisions of the Convention apply in relation to the domestic law of State P, that State may not tax the income in accordance with the provisions of the Convention; State R is thus under no obligation to exempt the income.

111. Such cases should not be confused with cases where the provisions of a Convention grant to the source State the right to tax an item of income but that item of income is not taxed under the domestic law of the State of source. In such cases, the State of residence must still exempt that item of income under the provisions of paragraph 1 of Article 23A (cf. paragraph 34 of the Commentary on Article 23).

112. Other cases that need to be distinguished are those where the double non-taxation results from disagreements between the State of residence and the State of source on the interpretation of the provisions of the Convention. In such cases, the State of residence does not agree that, in relation to the domestic law of the State of source, that State is precluded from taxing the item of income. The State of residence is therefore arguing that, to the extent that its interpretation of the Convention is correct, it has to grant exemption. Conversely, the source State is arguing that, if its interpretation of the Convention is the correct one, it cannot tax the income and the residence State should therefore not grant exemption. A similar problem could arise in the case of different interpretations of facts.

113. The Committee decided that the best way of addressing such cases of double non-taxation would be through a provision, to be added to Article 23A, that would provide that the residence State does not have to grant exemption in these cases. Such a provision would deal with cases of double non-taxation resulting from different interpretations of the provisions of the Convention or of the facts. The Committee therefore decided that the following paragraph 4 be added to Article 23A of the Model Tax Convention:

"4. The provisions of paragraph 1 shall not apply to income derived or capital owned by a resident of a Contracting State where the other Contracting State applies the provisions of this Convention to exempt such income or capital from tax or applies the provisions of paragraph 2 of Article 10 or 11 to such income."

114. This proposed provision would only apply to the extent that the State of source has applied the provisions of the Convention to exempt an item of income or capital or has applied the provisions of paragraph 2 of Article 10 or 11 to an item of income. The paragraph would therefore not apply where the State of source considers that it may tax an item of income or capital in accordance with the provisions of the Convention but where no tax is actually payable on such income or capital under the provisions of the domestic laws of the State of source. Similarly, where the source and residence States disagree not only with respect to the qualification of the income but also with respect to the amount of such income, paragraph 4 applies only to that part of the income that the State of source exempts from tax through the application of the Convention or to which that State applies paragraph 2 of Article 10 or 11.

115. The preceding comments concern the position of the residence State where the wording of the provisions on elimination of double taxation in the relevant bilateral Convention is similar to that of Article 23 of the Model Tax Convention. Where, however, the wording is different from that used in the Model Tax Convention, the result might also be different.

116. One variation that is often found in bilateral Convention is to begin the Article on elimination of double taxation by the words "[d]ouble taxation shall be avoided as follows: [...]". Where such wording is used, the conclusions presented in the preceding paragraphs would be reinforced since these words make it clear that the Article is intended to apply only where there is double taxation and the obligation imposed on the Contracting States to avoid double taxation will best be satisfied by adopting the approach described in this section.

117. In some Conventions, the Article on elimination of double taxation includes an explicit reference to internal law, e.g. requiring a credit for foreign taxes to be granted subject to the provisions of the domestic law regarding the crediting against domestic tax of tax payable in the other State but without affecting the general principle provided in the article. While the effect of these provisions has to be determined on the basis of their precise wording, such wording, which provides that the reference to domestic law should not affect the principle of the treaty article, will generally allow the application of the conclusions of the preceding paragraphs. In some Conventions, however, the reference to domestic law is not so limited, provided that any inconsistency between the domestic law and the treaty rules existed at the time of signature of the Convention. To avoid confusion, Contracting States may wish to make clear the extent to which domestic law will control in situations existing at the time of entry into force of the Convention where

APPLICATION OF THE MODEL TAX CONVENTION TO PARTNERSHIPS

the application of the domestic provision could be said to be inconsistent with the "general principle" of achieving double tax relief.

c)   *Cases of conflicts of qualification involving partnerships*

118.   The following examines how the general principles developed in the preceding subsection apply in some cases of conflicts of qualification involving partnerships.

119.   Starting with example 13 (the facts of that example appear in subsection a)), it should be concluded that in that example, the partial non-taxation referred to in paragraph 99 above will be avoided since State R will not be required to exempt what State P considers as interest since it may be said that State P may, under its domestic law, tax that part of the income of the partnership under paragraph 2 of Article 11. State R will therefore apply the credit method in that case, either under paragraph 2 of Article 23 A (exemption method) or under paragraph 1 of Article 23 B (credit method).

Example 15: *The facts are the same as in example 13 except that the treatment of the loan in States P and R is reversed. Partner A makes a loan to partnership P, which has been established in State P where it carries on a business through a permanent establishment. P pays interest to A. State R recognizes loans between partners and partnerships but State P does not. Both States treat partnerships as transparent entities and apply Article 7 to the income of P, but State R considers that Article 11 should apply to the payment made to partner A.*

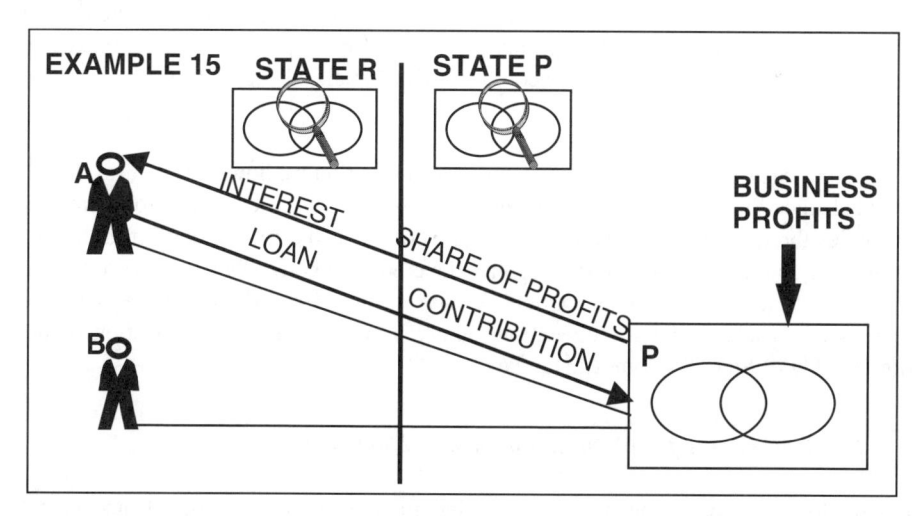

120.   This example is a mirror image of the conflict of qualification presented in example 13. State P, as the State of source of the income, determines that the payment is

a distribution of partner A's share of the partnership business profits and that Article 7 of the Convention applies to allow it to tax that share without restriction. State R, however, considers that the payment from P to A is a payment of interest subject to the rules of Article 11.

121. Again, the position of State P is in accordance with the provisions of the Convention. Pursuant to paragraph 2 of Article 3, State P has interpreted the words "debt-claims of every kind", which are found in paragraph 3 of Article 11, in accordance with its domestic law and has concluded that the financial contribution made by partner A did not qualify as a debt-claim for purposes of determining whether the payment was interest.

122. As Articles 23 A and 23 B both provide for the credit method to be applied in relation to interest, it may be argued that the consequences of that position for State R will be the same whether that State eliminates double taxation predominantly through the exemption method or through the credit method. Under the domestic law of State R, there is a debt-claim and partner A derives interest from State P. If State R follows that position when considering its obligation to eliminate double taxation under Articles 23 A or 23 B, that could lead it to consider that the payment made to partner A is interest that it may tax, subject to giving a credit for any State P tax levied in accordance with paragraph 2 of Article 11. If the Convention does not allow for source taxation of interest, the result of that approach will be double taxation. If the Convention follows Article 11 of the Model Tax Convention, the application of paragraph 2 of Articles 23 A or of paragraph 1 of Article 23 B under that approach will likely result in some double taxation to the extent that State R may only give credit for the part of the State P tax that it considers to have been imposed in accordance with Article 11, i.e. 10% of the payment of the interest.

123. On the basis of the principles developed in subsection b), however, that result will be avoided since State R will be obliged either to exempt what it considers to be interest (if it applies the exemption method) or to give a credit for the full amount of tax levied by State P on that item of income (if it applies the credit method). This is because the tax which State P has levied under Article 7 has been levied in accordance with the provisions of Article 7 of the Convention, taking into account the qualification of the income in light of State P's domestic tax law.

III.2   Problems arising from conflicts of income allocation

124. As discussed in section II, conflicts of income allocation may result from the fact that two Contracting States classify the same entity differently so that one treats it as a partnership and the other does not or from the fact that one State taxes partnerships as taxable entities while the other treats them as transparent entities for tax purposes. Such

APPLICATION OF THE MODEL TAX CONVENTION TO PARTNERSHIPS

conflicts, where the income is taxed by the two States in the hands of different taxpayers, create particular problems for the State of residence. These problems are discussed under the following examples.

Example 16: *P is a partnership established in State P. Partner B is a resident of State R while partner A is a resident of State P. State P treats the partnership as a taxable entity while State R treats it as a transparent entity. P derives royalty income from State R that is not attributable to a permanent establishment in State R. P has an office in State P and may therefore be considered to have a permanent establishment in State P.*

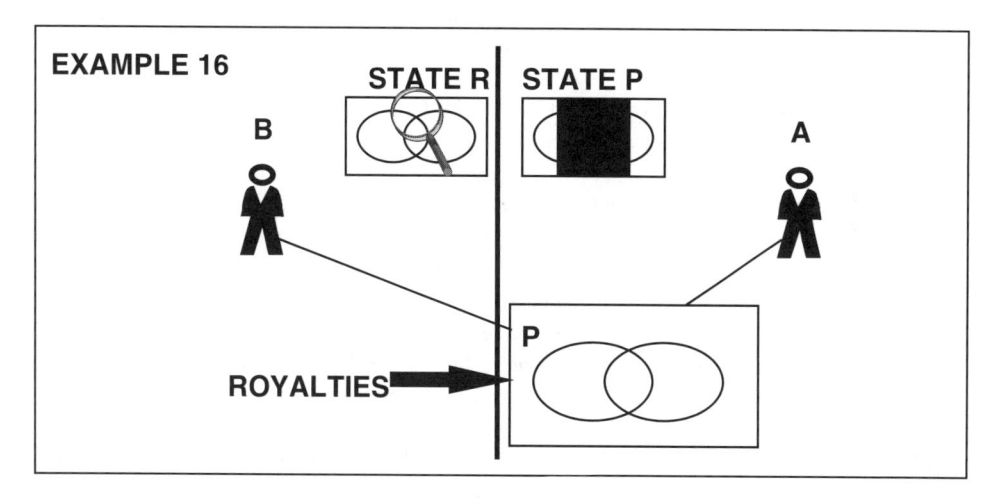

125. In that example, P qualifies as a resident of State P as it is a person "liable to tax" therein according to the laws of State P. Under Article 12 of the P-R treaty, it is clear that State R cannot tax the partnership on the royalty. State R, however, would like to tax partner B, a resident, on his share of the income of the partnership.

126. Some delegates took the position that the R-P Convention prevents State R from taxing in that situation. On the basis of paragraph 1 of Article 12, which provides that royalties arising in State R and paid to a resident of State P are taxable only in State P if the resident is the beneficial owner thereof, they argued that because the partnership qualifies as a resident of State P and is the beneficial owner of the royalties, the conditions of the paragraph are met and the royalties may only be taxed in State P. The delegates who adopted that interpretation therefore concluded that unless the case fell under the application of CFC rules or the Convention included a special provision allowing State R to tax its residents in such circumstances (e.g. a specific provision applicable to partnerships or a so-called "saving clause" such as is found in Conventions

concluded by the United States), the Convention would prevent State R from taxing partner B on his share of the royalties.

127. The majority, however, disagreed with that position. When taxing partner B, State R is taxing its own resident on income arising in its territory. Article 12 of the Convention does not affect taxation that is based on residence but only taxation that is based on source. When applying the Convention, State R may indeed consider, based on the principles developed in previous examples, that partner B may be considered to have received payment of his share of the royalties for the purposes of taxation in that State so that the limitation of Article 12 does not apply since that Article is only applicable where royalties arising in one State have been paid to a resident of the other State.

128. The Committee therefore decided that the Commentary on Article 1 be amended by adding the following paragraph thereto:

> "Where a partnership is treated as a resident of a Contracting State, the provisions of the Convention that restrict the other Contracting State's right to tax the partnership on its income do not apply to restrict that other State's right to tax the partners who are its own residents on their share of the income of the partnership. Some states may wish to include in their conventions a provision that expressly confirms a Contracting State's right to tax resident partners on their share of the income of a partnership that is treated as a resident of the other State."

129. Since State R's right to tax partner B on his share of the income of the partnership derives from the partner's residence in that State, it follows that State R must also give the benefits of Article 23 to partner B. The fact that the partnership has a permanent establishment in State P is not relevant in that respect since, as discussed in subsection b), the tax levied by State P will still have been levied in accordance with the provisions of the Convention since State P is allowed to tax partnership P as its resident. The application of Article 23 by State R may, however, raise some difficulties because State P will levy its tax on the partnership rather than on the partners and because that tax may be levied both when the income is realized and when it is distributed (i.e. through a withholding tax on the distribution which State P may treat as a dividend). These difficulties are examined below in relation to example 18.

APPLICATION OF THE MODEL TAX CONVENTION TO PARTNERSHIPS

Example 17: *P is a partnership established in State P. A and B are P's partners who reside in State R. State P treats P as a taxable entity while State R treats it as a transparent entity. P derives royalty income from State P that is not attributable to a permanent establishment in that state.*

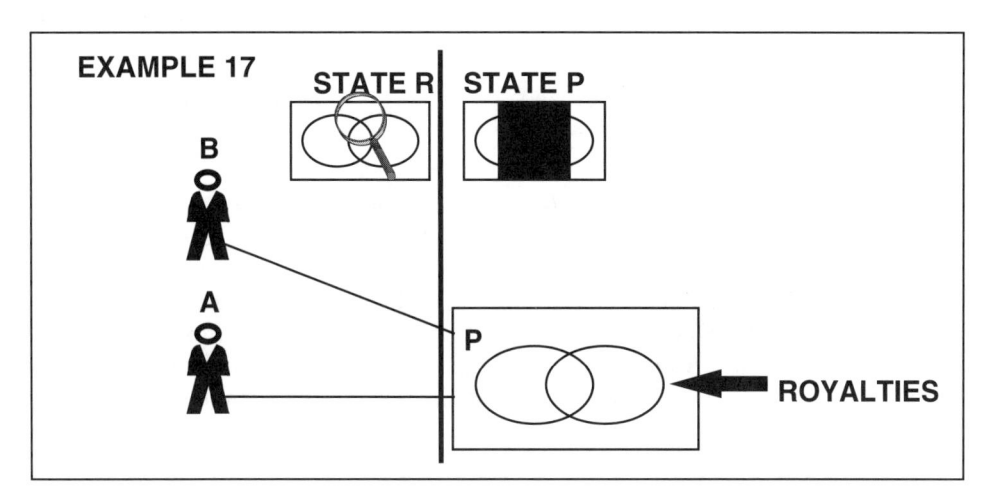

130. This example addresses a factual situation similar to that described in the preceding example but from the perspective of the State of residence of the partnership, i.e. State P. In this example, State P would, under its domestic law, impose tax on the royalties in the hands of the partnership. From its perspective, P is a resident taxpayer and as such liable to tax on its income arising in State P. Thus, Article 12 of the Convention would not apply since the royalties arise in State P and are paid to a resident of State P. However, because State R allocates the income to partners A and B, they are also liable to tax on the royalties in State R as residents. There would thus be double taxation on the same item of income because of the differing allocation rules in this situation.

131. The majority was of the view that, despite the general principles discussed in Section II.5 which would require the source State to take into consideration the treatment of the income in the State of the residence of the partners, in this situation State P would not be limited in its taxing rights by the P-R Convention. In its view, the situation involves a purely domestic matter from the perspective of State P; it is simply taxing the domestic source income of a resident taxpayer and nothing in the Convention can limit that right. The fact that double taxation results because of the differing income allocations of States R and P is not a reason to limit its right to tax its residents.

132. Some delegates, however, would continue to follow the principle that State P, in applying the Convention, should take into account the fact that, under the allocation of income rules in State R, the income would be liable to tax in the hands of A and B. Their position would be that State P is obliged to relieve the potential resulting double taxation by applying Article 12 to exempt the income in the hands of the partners, thus leaving the exclusive taxing right with State R.

133. Where P continues to tax the income in the hands of P, the possible application of Article 23 is discussed in section III.1.

Example 18: *In Year 1, P, which is established and has a permanent establishment in State P, earns profits of 1 million. In Year 2, P distributes to A, a resident of State R, his share in the profits earned in Year 1 (300,000). Under State P's domestic law, P is a company, and the profits would be taxed in Year 1 at 40% (400,000). In year 2, a further withholding tax (30,000) on the distribution to A would be imposed (by treating it as a dividend). Under State R's domestic law, P is fiscally transparent, and State R would tax A in Year 1 on A's share in P's profits (500,000). State R would treat the distribution in year 2 as having no tax effect.*

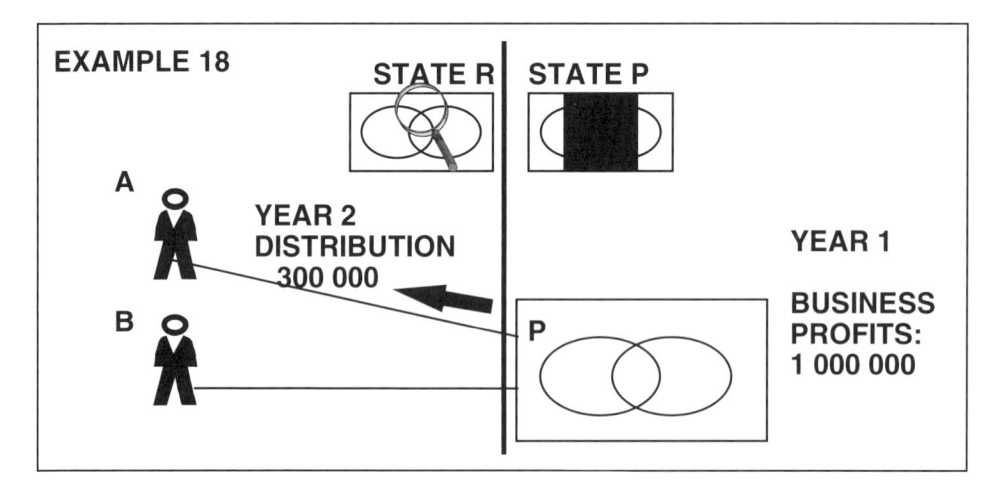

134. In this example, the conflict in income allocation that results from the different treatment of partnerships in States P and R raises the following various difficulties with respect to the elimination of double taxation by State R:

- the fact that State P taxes two different events (the earning of the profits and their distribution) while State R only taxes one event (the earning of the profits);

- the timing mismatch that results from the fact that State P taxes the distribution in year 2 but State R imposes its tax in year 1;

- the fact that the State P tax which is levied when the profits are earned is paid by the partnership while the State R tax is levied on the partners.

135. The first difficulty relates to whether State R should provide credit for the tax levied by State P upon the distribution. This is an issue that concerns equally States applying the exemption method and States applying the credit method. If State R applies the exemption method, it must refrain from taxing the partnership's business profits derived from State P in year 1 (it is, of course, entitled to take the excluded income into account in determining the rate of tax on A's remaining income pursuant to paragraph 3 of Article 23 A); if it is a credit State, it must give credit for State P's tax levied on these profits in year 1. In both cases, however, the Convention theoretically requires that it should provide a credit for State P's tax levied on the distribution against its tax on such a distribution (paragraph 2 of Article 23 A and paragraph 1 of Article 23 B).

136. Since, however, State R does not tax the distribution, there is no tax levied by State R against which to credit State P's tax levied upon the distribution. While the Convention would allow State R to tax the profit distribution made in year 2, such taxation would be inconsistent with State R's treatment of partnership and is therefore not allowed by its domestic law. Under that law, the income may be taxed (subject to any relief from double taxation) only in the year it was earned, i.e. year 1. The manner in which taxation rights allowed by a treaty are exercised is, of course, a matter of domestic law.

137. A clear distinction must be made between the generation of profits and the distribution of those profits. State R, if it is an exemption State, has to exempt from tax the generation of profits in year 1 and therefore is not permitted under the Convention to tax the profits when earned on the basis that Article 10 would allow them to be taxed when distributed. Similarly, however, State R (if it is a credit State) should not be expected to credit the tax levied by State P upon distribution against its own tax levied upon generation.

138. Once it is agreed that State R does not levy tax on the distribution, the second difficulty, i.e. the timing mismatch, is no longer relevant. While timing mismatches frequently create problems for foreign tax credit purposes, which leads States to adopt rules allowing for the carry-back or carry-forward of foreign tax credits, the issue does not arise in this example since there is no double taxation of the distribution.

139. The third difficulty concerns only States that apply the credit method and relates to the fact that both States impose tax upon the same income, but on different taxpayers. The issue is therefore whether State R, which taxes partner A on his share in the

partnership profits, is obliged, under the Convention, to give credit for the source tax that is levied in State P on partnership P, which State P treats as a separate taxable entity. The answer to that question must be affirmative. To the extent that State R flows-through the income of the partnership to the partners for the purpose of taxing them, it should be consistent and flow-through the tax paid by the partnership for the purposes of eliminating double taxation arising from its taxation of the partners. In other words, if the corporate status given to the partnership by State P is ignored for purposes of taxing the share in the profits, it should likewise be ignored for purposes of giving access to the foreign tax credit.

ANNEX I: PROPOSED CHANGES TO THE OECD MODEL TAX CONVENTION

The following are the changes to the Model Tax Convention resulting from the report (changes to the existing text of the Commentary are indicated by ***bold italics*** and ~~strikethrough~~):

Articles of the Model

1. Add the following paragraph 4 to Article 23A of the Model Tax Convention:

    "4. The provisions of paragraph 1 shall not apply to income derived or capital owned by a resident of a Contracting State where the other Contracting State applies the provisions of this Convention to exempt such income or capital from tax or applies the provisions of paragraph 2 of Article 10 or 11 to such income."

Commentary

2. Delete paragraphs 2 to 6 of the Commentary on Article 1 and replace them by the following:

    "2. Domestic laws differ in the treatment of partnerships. These differences create various difficulties when applying tax Conventions in relation to partnerships. These difficulties are analysed in the report by the Committee on Fiscal Affairs entitled "The application of the OECD Model Tax Convention to Partnerships", the conclusions of which have been incorporated below and in the Commentary on various other provisions of the Model Tax Convention.

    3. [FROM PARA. 2] *As discussed in that report, a main source of difficulties is* the fact that some countries treat partnerships as taxable units (sometimes even as companies) whereas other countries ***adopt what may be referred to as the fiscally transparent approach, under which the partnership is ignored for tax purposes*** and the individual partners ***are taxed*** on their respective share of the partnership's income.

    4. *A first difficulty is the extent to which a partnership is entitled as such to the benefits of the provisions of the Convention. Under Article 1, only persons who are residents of the Contracting States are entitled to the benefits of the tax*

Convention entered into by these States. While paragraph 2 of the Commentary on Article 3 explains why a partnership constitutes a person, a partnership does not necessarily qualify as a resident of a Contracting State under Article 4.

5. [FROM PARA. 3] Where a partnership is treated as a company or taxed in the same way, it ~~may reasonably be argued that the partnership~~ is a resident of the Contracting State ~~taxing~~ *that taxes* the partnership on the grounds mentioned in paragraph 1 of Article 4 and, therefore, ~~falling under the scope of the Convention,~~ *it* is entitled to the benefits of the Convention. ~~In the other instances mentioned in paragraph 2 above, the application of the Convention to the partnership as such might be refused, at least if no special rule covering partnerships is provided for in the Convention.~~ *Where, however, a partnership is treated as fiscally transparent in a State, the partnership is not "liable to tax" in that State within the meaning of paragraph 1 of Article 4, and so cannot be a resident thereof for purposes of the Convention. In such a case, the application of the Convention to the partnership as such would be refused, unless a special rule covering partnerships were provided for in the Convention. Where the application of the Convention is so refused, the partners should be entitled, with respect to their share of the income of the partnership, to the benefits provided by the Conventions entered into by the States of which they are residents to the extent that the partnership's income is allocated to them for the purposes of taxation in their State of residence (cf. paragraph 8.2 of the Commentary on Article 4).*

6. The relationship between the partnership's entitlement to the benefits of a tax Convention and that of the partners raises other questions.

6.1 One issue is the effect that the application of the provisions of the Convention to a partnership can have on the taxation of the partners. Where a partnership is treated as a resident of a Contracting State, the provisions of the Convention that restrict the other Contracting State's right to tax the partnership on its income do not apply to restrict that other State's right to tax the partners who are its own residents on their share of the income of the partnership. Some states may wish to include in their conventions a provision that expressly confirms a Contracting State's right to tax resident partners on their share of the income of a partnership that is treated as a resident of the other State.

6.2 Another issue is that of the effect of the provisions of the Convention on a Contracting State's right to tax income arising on its territory where the entitlement to the benefits of one, or more than one, Conventions is different for the partners and the partnership. Where, for instance, the State of source treats a domestic partnership as fiscally transparent and therefore taxes the partners on their share of the income of the partnership, a partner that is resident of a State that taxes partnerships as companies would not be able to claim the benefits of the Convention between the two States with respect to the share of the partnership's income that the State of source taxes in his hands since that income, though allocated to the person claiming the benefits of the Convention under the laws of the State of source, is not similarly allocated for purposes of determining the liability to tax on that item of income in the State of residence of that person.

6.3 The results described in the preceding paragraph should obtain even if, as a matter of the domestic law of the State of source, the partnership would not be regarded as transparent for tax purposes but as a separate taxable entity to which the income would be attributed, provided that the partnership is not actually considered as a resident of the State of source. This conclusion is founded upon the principle that the State of source should take into account, as part of the factual context in which the Convention is to be applied, the way in which an item of income, arising in its jurisdiction, is treated in the jurisdiction of the person claiming the benefits of the Convention as a resident. For States which could not agree with this interpretation of the Article, it would be possible to provide for this result in a special provision which would avoid the resulting potential double taxation where the income of the partnership is differently allocated by the two States.

6.4 Where, as described in paragraphs 6.2, income has "flowed through" a transparent partnership to the partners who are liable to tax on that income in the State of their residence then the income is appropriately viewed as "paid" to the partners since it is to them and not to the partnership that the income is allocated for purposes of determining their tax liability in their State of residence. Hence the partners, in these circumstances, satisfy the condition, imposed in several Articles, that the income concerned is "paid to a resident of the other Contracting State". Similarly the requirement, imposed by some other Articles, that income or gains are "derived by a resident of the other Contracting State" is met in the circumstances described above. This interpretation avoids denying the benefits of tax Conventions to a partnership's income on the basis that neither the partnership, because it is not a resident, nor the partners, because the income is not directly paid to them or derived by them, can claim the benefits of the Convention with respect to that income. Following from the principle discussed in paragraph 6.3, the conditions that the income be paid to, or derived by, a resident should be considered to be satisfied even where, as a matter of the domestic law of the State of s ource, the partnership would not be regarded as transparent for tax purposes, provided that the partnership is not actually considered as a resident of the State of source.

6.5 Partnership cases involving three States pose difficult problems with respect to the determination of entitlement to benefits under Conventions. However, many problems may be solved through the application of the principles described in paragraphs 6.2 to 6.4. Where a partner is a resident of one State, the partnership is established in another State and the partner shares in partnership income arising in a third State then the partner may claim the benefits of the Convention between his State of residence and the State of source of the income to the extent that the partnership's income is allocated to him for the purposes of taxation in his State of residence. If, in addition, the partnership is taxed as a resident of the State in which it is established then the partnership may itself claim the benefits of the Convention between the State in which it is established and the State of source. In such a case of "double benefits", the State of source may not impose taxation which is inconsistent with the terms of either applicable Convention therefore, where different rates are provided for in the two Conventions, the lower will be applied. However, Contracting States may wish to consider special provisions to deal with the administration of benefits under Conventions in situations such as these, so that the partnership may claim benefits but partners could not present concurrent claims. Such provisions could ensure appropriate and simplified administration of the giving of benefits. No benefits will be available under the Convention between the State in which the partnership is established and the State of source if the partnership is regarded as transparent for tax purposes by the State in which it is established. Similarly no benefits will be available under the Convention between the State of residence of the partner and the State of source if the income of the partnership is not allocated to the partner under the taxation law of the State of residence. If the partnership is regarded as transparent for tax purposes by the State in which it is established and the income of the partnership is not allocated to the partner under the taxation law of the State of residence of the partner, the State of source may tax partnership income allocable to the partner without restriction.

6.6 Differences in how countries apply the fiscally transparent approach may create other difficulties for the application of tax Conventions. Where a State considers that a partnership does not qualify as a resident of a Contracting State because it is not liable to tax and the partners are liable to tax in their State of residence on their share of the partnership's income, it is expected that that State will apply the provisions of the Convention as if the partners had earned the income directly so that the classification of the income for purposes of the allocative rules of Articles 6 to 21 will not be modified by the fact that the income flows-through the partnership. Difficulties may arise, however, in the application of provisions which refer to the activities of the taxpayer, the nature of the taxpayer, the relationship between the taxpayer and another party to a transaction. Some of these difficulties are discussed in paragraphs 19.1 of the Commentary on Article 5 and paragraphs 6.1 and 6.2 of the Commentary on Article 15.

APPLICATION OF THE MODEL TAX CONVENTION TO PARTNERSHIPS

6.7 Finally a number of other difficulties arise where different rules of the Convention are applied by the Contracting States to income derived by a partnership or its partners, depending on the domestic laws of these States or their interpretation of the provisions of the Convention or of the relevant facts. These difficulties relate to the broader issue of conflicts of qualification, which is dealt with in paragraphs 32.1 ff. and 56.1 ff. of the Commentary on Article 23."

3. Delete the last sentence of paragraph 2 of the Commentary on Article 3 and replace it by the following:

"Partnerships will also be considered to be "persons" either because they fall within the definition of "company" or, where this is not the case, because they constitute other bodies of persons."

4. Add the following paragraph 10.1 to the Commentary on Article 3:

"10.1 The separate mention of partnerships in sub-paragraph 1 f) is not inconsistent with the status of a partnership as a person under sub-paragraph 1 a). Under the domestic laws of some countries, it is possible for an entity to be a "person" but not a "legal person" for tax purposes. The explicit statement is necessary to avoid confusion."

5. Add the following paragraph 8.2 to the Commentary on Article 4:

"8.2 Where a State disregards a partnership for tax purposes and treats it as fiscally transparent, taxing the partners on their share of the partnership income, the partnership itself is not liable to tax and may not, therefore, be considered to be a resident of that State. In such a case, since the income of the partnership "flows through" to the partners under the domestic law of that State, the partners are the persons who are liable to tax on that income and are thus the appropriate persons to claim the benefits of the Conventions concluded by the States of which they are residents. This latter result will obtain even if, under the domestic law of the State of source, the income is attributed to a partnership which is treated as a separate taxable entity. For States which could not agree with this interpretation of the Article, it would be possible to provide for this result in a special provision which would avoid the resulting potential double taxation where the income of the partnership is differently allocated by the two States."

6. Add the following paragraph 19.1 to the Commentary on Article 5:

"19.1 In the case of fiscally transparent partnerships, the twelve month test is applied at the level of the partnership as concerns its own activities. If the period of time spent on the site by the partners and the employees of the partnership

exceeds twelve month, the enterprise carried on by the partnership will therefore be considered to have a permanent establishment. Each partner will thus be considered to have a permanent establishment for purposes of the taxation of his share of the business profits derived by the partnership regardless of the time spent by himself on the site."

7. Renumber paragraph 7 of the Commentary on Article 15 as paragraph 6 and add the following paragraphs 6.1 and 6.2:

"6.1 The application of the second condition in the case of fiscally transparent partnerships present difficulties since such partnerships cannot qualify as a resident of a Contracting State under Article 4 (cf. paragraph 8.2 of the Commentary on Article 4). While it is clear that such a partnership could qualify as an "employer" (especially under the domestic law definitions of the term in some countries, e.g. where an employer is defined as a person liable for a wage tax), the application of the condition at the level of the partnership regardless of the situation of the partners would therefore render the condition totally meaningless.

6.2 The object and purpose of subparagraphs 2b) and c) of paragraph 2 are to avoid the source taxation of short-term employments to the extent that the employment income is not allowed as a deductible expense in the State of source because the employer is not taxable in that State as he neither is a resident nor has a permanent establishment therein. These subparagraphs can also be justified by the fact that imposing source deduction requirements with respect to short-term employments in a given State may be considered to be constitute an excessive administrative burden where the employer neither resides nor has a permanent establishment in that State. In order to achieve a meaningful interpretation of subparagraph 2b) that would accord with its context and its object, it should therefore be considered that, in the case of fiscally transparent partnerships, that subparagraph applies at the level of the partners. Thus, the concepts of "employer" and "resident", as found in subparagraph 2b), are applied at the level of the partners rather than at the level of a fiscally transparent partnership. This approach is consistent with that under which other provisions of tax Conventions must be applied at the partners' rather than at the partnership's level. While this interpretation could create difficulties where the partners reside in different States, such difficulties could be addressed through the mutual agreement procedure by determining, for example, the State in which the partners who own the majority of the interests in the partnership reside (i.e. the State in which the greatest part of the deduction will be claimed)."

8. Add the following heading and paragraphs immediately after paragraph 32 of the Commentary on Article 23:

APPLICATION OF THE MODEL TAX CONVENTION TO PARTNERSHIPS

"E. *Conflicts of qualification*[1]

32.1 Both Articles 23 A and 23 B require that relief be granted, through the exemption or credit method, as the case may be, where an item of income or capital may be taxed by the State of source in accordance with the provisions of the Convention. Thus, the State of residence has the obligation to apply the exemption or credit method in relation to an item of income or capital where the Convention authorizes taxation of that item by the State of source.

32.2 The interpretation of the phrase "in accordance with the provisions of this Convention, may be taxed", which is used in both Articles, is particularly important when dealing with cases where the State of residence and the State of source classify the same item of income or capital differently for purposes of the provisions of the Convention.

32.3 Different situations need to be considered in that respect. Where, due to differences in the domestic law between the State of source and the State of residence, the former applies, with respect to a particular item of income or capital, provisions of the Convention that are different from those that the State of residence would have applied to the same item of income or capital, the income is still being taxed in accordance with the provisions of the Convention, as interpreted and applied by the State of source. In such a case, therefore, the two Articles require that relief from double taxation be granted by the State of residence notwithstanding the conflict of qualification resulting from these differences in domestic law.

32.4 This point may be illustrated by the following example. A business is carried on through a permanent establishment in State E by a partnership established in that State. A partner, resident in State R, alienates his interest in that partnership. State E treats the partnership as fiscally transparent whereas State R treats it as taxable entity. State E therefore considers that the alienation of the interest in the partnership is, for the purposes of its Convention with State R, an alienation by the partner of the underlying assets of the business carried on by the partnership, which may be taxed by that State in accordance with paragraph 1 or 2 of Article 13. State R, as it treats the partnership as a taxable entity, considers that the alienation of the interest in the partnership is akin to the alienation of a share in a company, which could not be taxed by State E by reason of paragraph 4 of Article 13. In such a case, the conflict of qualification results exclusively from the different treatment of partnerships in the domestic laws of the two States and State E must be considered by State R to have taxed the

---

1. See the diverging opinion by Switzerland in Annex II.

gain from the alienation "in accordance with the provisions of the Convention" for purposes of the application of Article 23 A or Article 23 B. State R must therefore grant an exemption pursuant to Article 23 A or give a credit pursuant to Article 23 B irrespective of the fact that, under its own domestic law, it treats the alienation gain as income from the disposition of shares in a corporate entity and that, if State E's qualification of the income were consistent with that of State R, State R would not have to give relief under Article 23 A or Article 23 B. No double taxation will therefore arise in such a case.

32.5   *Article 23 A and Article 23 B, however, do not require that the State of residence eliminate double taxation in all cases where the State of source has imposed its tax by applying to an item of income a provision of the Convention that is different from that which the State of residence considers to be applicable. For instance, in the example above, if, for purposes of applying paragraph 2 of Article 13, State E considers that the partnership carried on business through a fixed place of business but State R considers that paragraph 4 applies because the partnership did not have a fixed place of business in State E, there is actually a dispute as to whether State E has taxed the income in accordance with the provisions of the Convention. The same may be said if State E, when applying paragraph 2 of Article 13, interprets the phrase "forming part of the business property" so as to include certain assets which would not fall within the meaning of that phrase according to the interpretation given to it by State R. Such conflicts resulting from different interpretation of facts or different interpretation of the provisions of the Convention must be distinguished from the conflicts of qualification described in the above paragraph where the divergence is based not on different interpretations of the provisions of the Convention but on different provisions of domestic law. In the former case, State R can argue that State E has not imposed its tax in accordance with the provisions of the Convention if it has applied its tax based on what State R considers to be a wrong interpretation of the facts or a wrong interpretation of the Convention. States should use the provisions of Article 25 (Mutual Agreement Procedure), and in particular paragraph 3 thereof, in order to resolve this type of conflict in cases that would otherwise result in unrelieved double taxation.*

32.6   *The phrase "in accordance with the provisions of this Convention, may be taxed" must also be interpreted in relation to possible cases of double non-taxation that can arise under Article 23 A. Where the State of source considers that the provisions of the Convention preclude it from taxing an item of income or capital which it would otherwise have taxed, the State of residence should, for purposes of applying paragraph 1 of Article 23 A, consider that the item of income may not be taxed by the State of source in accordance with the provisions of the Convention, even though the State of residence would have applied the Convention differently so as to tax that income if it had been in the position of* the State of source. Thus the State of residence is not required by paragraph 1 to exempt the item of income, a result which is consistent with the basic function of Article 23 which is to eliminate double taxation.

32.7 This situation may be illustrated by reference to a variation of the example described above. A business is carried on through a fixed place of business in State E by a partnership established in that State and a partner, resident in State R, alienates his interest in that partnership. Changing the facts of the example, however, it is now assumed that State E treats the partnership as a taxable entity whereas State R treats it as fiscally transparent; it is further assumed that State R is a State that applies the exemption method. State E, as it treats the partnership as a corporate entity, considers that the alienation of the interest in the partnership is akin to the alienation of a share in a company, which it cannot tax by reason of paragraph 4 of Article 13. State R, on the other hand, considers that the alienation of the interest in the partnership should have been taxable by State E as an alienation by the partner of the underlying assets of the business carried on by the partnership to which paragraphs 1 or 2 of Article 13 would have been applicable. In determining whether it has the obligation to exempt the income under paragraph 1 of Article 23 A, State R should nonetheless consider that, given the way that the provisions of the Convention apply in conjunction with the domestic law of State E, that State may not tax the income in accordance with the provisions of the Convention. State R is thus under no obligation to exempt the income."

9. Replace paragraphs 34 to 36 of the Commentary on Article 23 by the following:

"34. The State of residence must accordingly *exempt income and capital which may be taxed by the other State in* accordance *with the Convention* whether or not the right to tax is in effect exercised by *that* other State. This method is regarded as the most practical one since it relieves the State of residence from undertaking investigations of the actual taxation position in the other State.

34.1 The obligation imposed on the State of residence to exempt a particular item of income or capital depends on whether this item may be taxed by the State of source in accordance with the Convention. Paragraphs 32.1 to 32.7 above discuss how this condition should be interpreted. Where the condition is met, however, the obligation may be considered as absolute, subject to the exceptions of paragraphs 2 and 4 of Article 23 A. Paragraph 2 addresses the case, already mentioned in paragraph 31 above, of items of income which may only be subjected to a limited tax in the State of source. For such items of income, the paragraph provides for the credit method (cf. paragraph 47 below). Paragraph 4 addresses the case of certain conflicts of qualification which would result in double non-taxation as a consequence of the application of the Convention if the

State of residence were obliged to give exemption (cf. paragraphs 56.1 to 56.3 below).

35. Occasionally, negotiating States may find it reasonable in certain circumstances, *in order to avoid double non-taxation*, to make an exception to the absolute obligation on the State of residence to give *exemption in cases where neither paragraph 3 nor 4 would apply*. Such may be the case *where no tax on specific items of income or capital is provided under the domestic laws of the State of source, or* tax is not effectively collected owing to special circumstances such as the set-off of losses, a mistake, or the statutory time limit having expired. To avoid *such* double non-taxation of specific items of income, Contracting States may agree to amend the relevant Article itself (cf. paragraph 9 of the Commentary on Article 15 and paragraph 12 of the Commentary on Article 17; for the converse case where relief in the State of source is subject to actual taxation in the State of residence, cf. paragraph 20 of the Commentary on Article 10, paragraph 10 of the Commentary on Article 11, paragraph 6 of the Commentary on Article 12, paragraph 21 of the Commentary on Article 13 and paragraph 3 of the Commentary on Article 21). One might also make an exception to the general rule, in order to achieve a certain reciprocity, where one of the States adopts the exemption method and the other the credit method. Finally, another exception to the general rule may be made where a State wishes to apply to specific items of income the credit method rather than exemption (cf. paragraph 31 above).

36. ~~As already mentioned in paragraph 31 above, the exemption method does not apply to such items of income which according to the Convention may be taxed in the State of residence but may also be subjected to a limited tax in the other Contracting State. For such items of income, paragraph 2 of Article 23 A provides for the credit method (cf. paragraph 47 below)."~~

10. Add the following heading and paragraphs immediately after paragraph 56 of the Commentary on Article 23:

"*Paragraph 4*

56.1 The purpose of this paragraph is to avoid double non taxation as a result of disagreements between the State of residence and the State of source on the facts of a case or on the interpretation of the provisions of the Convention. The paragraph applies where, on the one hand, the State of source interprets the facts of a case or the provisions of the Convention in such a way that an item of income or capital falls under a provision of the Convention that eliminates its right to tax that item or limits the tax that it can impose while, on the other hand, the State of residence adopts a different interpretation of the facts or of the provisions of the Convention and thus considers that the item may be taxed in the

APPLICATION OF THE MODEL TAX CONVENTION TO PARTNERSHIPS

State of source in accordance with the Convention, which, absent this paragraph, would lead to an obligation for the State of residence to give exemption under the provisions of paragraph 1.

56.2 The paragraph only applies to the extent that the State of source has applied the provisions of the Convention to exempt an item of income or capital or has applied the provisions of paragraph 2 of Article 10 or 11 to an item of income. The paragraph would therefore not apply where the State of source considers that it may tax an item of income or capital in accordance with the provisions of the Convention but where no tax is actually payable on such income or capital under the provisions of the domestic laws of the State of source. In such a case, the State of residence must exempt that item of income under the provisions of paragraph 1 because the exemption in the State of source does not result from the application of the provisions of the Convention but, rather, from the domestic law of the State of source (cf. paragraph 34 above). Similarly, where the source and residence States disagree not only with respect to the qualification of the income but also with respect to the amount of such income, paragraph 4 applies only to that part of the income that the State of source exempts from tax through the application of the Convention or to which that State applies paragraph 2 of Article 10 or 11.

56.3 Cases where the paragraph apply must be distinguished from cases where the qualification of an item of income under the domestic law of the State of source interacts with the provisions of the Convention to preclude that State from taxing an item of income or capital in circumstances where the qualification of that item under the domestic law of the State of residence would not have had the same result. In such a case, which is discussed in paragraphs 32.6 and 32.7 above, paragraph 1 does not impose an obligation on the State of residence to give exemption because the item of income may not be taxed in the State of source in accordance with the Convention. Since paragraph 1 does not apply, the provisions of paragraph 4 are not required in such a case to ensure the taxation right of the State of residence."

11. Replace paragraph 59 of the Commentary on Article 23 by the following:

"59. The obligation imposed by Article 23 B on a State R to give credit for the tax levied in the other State E (or S) on an item of income or capital depends on whether this item may be taxed by the State E (or S) in accordance with the Convention. Paragraphs 32.1 to 32.7 above discuss how this condition should be interpreted. ~~It is to be noted that Article 23 B applies in a State R only to items of income or capital which, in accordance with the Convention, "may be taxed" in the other State E (or S).~~ Items of income or capital which according to Article 8, to paragraph 3 of Article 13, to sub-paragraph a) of paragraphs 1 and 2 of Article 19 and to paragraph 3 of Article 22, "shall be taxable only" in the other State, are from the outset exempt from tax in State R (cf. paragraph 6 above), and the Commentary on Article 23 A applies to such exempted income and capital. As regards progression, reference is made to paragraph 2 of the Article (and paragraph 79 below).

12. Add the following paragraphs 69.1 to 69.3 to the Commentary on Article 23:

"69.1 Problems may arise where Contracting States treat entities such as partnerships in a different way. Assume, for example, that the State of source treats a partnership as a company and the State of residence of a partner treats it as fiscally transparent. The State of source may, subject to the applicable provisions of the Convention, tax the partnership on its income when that income is realized and, subject to the limitations of paragraph 2 of Article 10, may also tax the distribution of profits by the partnership to its non-resident partners. The State of residence, however, will only tax the partner on his share of the partnership's income when that income is realized by the partnership.

69.2 The first issue that arises in this case is whether the State of residence, which taxes the partner on his share in the partnership's income, is obliged, under the Convention, to give credit for the tax that is levied in the State of source on the partnership, which that latter State treats as a separate taxable entity. The answer to that question must be affirmative. To the extent that the State of residence flows-through the income of the partnership to the partner for the purpose of taxing him, it must adopt a coherent approach and flow-through to the partner the tax paid by the partnership for the purposes of eliminating double taxation arising from its taxation of the partner. In other words, if the corporate status given to the partnership by the State of source is ignored by the State of residence for purposes of taxing the partner on his share of the income, it should likewise be ignored for purposes of the foreign tax credit.

69.3 A second issue that arises in this case is the extent to which the State of residence must provide credit for the tax levied by the State of source on the distribution, which is not taxed in the State of residence. The answer to that question lies in that last fact. Since the distribution is not taxed in the State of residence, there is simply no tax in the State of residence against which to credit the tax levied by the State of source upon the distribution. A clear distinction must be made between the generation of profits and the distribution of those profits and the State of residence should not be expected to credit the tax levied by the State of source upon the distribution against its own tax levied upon generation (cf. the first sentence of paragraph 64 above)."

ANNEX II: RESERVATIONS BY FRANCE, GERMANY, THE NETHERLANDS, PORTUGAL AND SWITZERLAND

France

1. France considers that the criteria mentioned in paragraphs 40 to 42 in order to decide whether a partnership is "liable to tax" or not are not sufficient to take into account situations where a partnership is partly treated as a taxable unit and partly disregarded for tax purposes.

2. For the purposes of French tax law, a partnership would always be regarded as liable to tax, even if in fact taxation is applied not against the partnership as such but on the partners on behalf of the partnership according to the share corresponding to their participation in the partnership.

3. Consequently, France does not share the conclusions of Section II.3 *b)*.

4. France also disagrees with the conclusions mentioned in paragraph 35 under which, if the application of the Convention to the partnership is refused, the partners would always be entitled to the benefits provided by the Convention entered into by the countries of which they are residents. The opinion of France is that such a solution depends to some extent upon the provisions included in the Convention concluded with the State where the partnership is situated.

5. The implications of the above comments with regard to the introductory examples examined in sections II.4 and II.5 are as follows:

A. *France considers that it is not appropriate to refer to a single criterion to determine whether a partnership is "liable to tax".*

6. The systems which different States use to impose tax on partnerships and their constituent partners are highly complex.

7. It is not sufficient to note that the amount of tax due payable on the partnership income is determined in relation to the personal characteristics of the partners to conclude that the partnership should not itself be considered to be "liable to tax".

8. The use of such reasoning to determine whether the provisions of Conventions are applicable is likely to lead to a situation in which some States are placed in the category of those which apply a fiscally transparent approach to partnerships despite the fact their own domestic legislation considers such entities to be liable to tax.

9. If this line of reasoning were to be pursued further, then despite the fact that under French tax law a partnership is always considered to be liable to tax France would have to be classified among those States which do not recognise their own partnerships are being "resident" within the meaning of the report.

10. To the extent that it does not recognise itself as a State which treats partnerships as being fiscally transparent, France cannot endorse the conclusions of the Committee with regard to the examples presented in section II.4.

11. In example 2, for instance, France's opinion, in the event that it were State P in which the partnership was established, is that:

– firstly, the partnership, given that it is liable to tax, is entitled to claim the benefits of the Convention;

– secondly, the applicable Convention is that between S and P and not the one between S and R.

B. *France does not share the view that in cases where the application of the Convention is denied to a partnership the members of that partnership may claim the benefits of the Conventions entered into by the States of which they are residents by virtue of the fact that they are liable to tax in those States on their share of the partnership income.*

12. Even when the partnership is established in a State which applies a fiscally transparent approach, the fact that the partnership is a legal person precludes the view that income simply "flows through" this entity to the partners.

13. Since a partnership constitutes a separate legal entity, it cannot be ignored for tax purposes.

14. Although treating partnerships as being liable to tax, France therefore cannot agree with the conclusions reached by the Committee with regard to the examples reviewed in section II.5.

15. In example 4, for instance, were France to be placed in the position of State S, it would refuse to apply the provisions of the Convention with State P because the fact that the partnership was not liable to tax in the State in which it was established would preclude it from claiming the benefits of the Convention.

16. We therefore cannot approve the proposed amendment of the Commentary on Article 1 in the Model Tax Convention with regard to the new paragraphs 6.5, 6.6 and 8.2 (Annex 1 of the report).

Administrative difficulties

17. Furthermore, France considers that the administrative difficulties with regard to implementation noted in example 9 (partnerships with many partners residing in different States), the problems regarding the flow in information mentioned in example 10 (partnership established in a State which does not have a tax convention with the source State, which nonetheless has signed a Convention with the State of which the partners are residents), and the risks of double-exemptions in triangular cases in which the State of residence of the partners and the State in which the partnership has its head office apply the principle of transparency are of a such a nature as to invalidate the solution whereby the partnership is disregarded in order to allow the partners to benefit from application of the Convention.

Germany

Observations by Germany on paragraph 45

18. Germany does not share the views expressed in paragraph 45. Under the special provisions mentioned in paragraph 43 one may have to determine when the income is attributable to a permanent establishment in the State of the partnership or in a third State, but this is not more difficult with respect to a partnership than in other instances where it has to be determined whether income is effectively connected with a permanent establishment. How the reduction of a withholding tax should be calculated where only a "part" of the partnership is treated as a treaty resident may not always be clear. But as a rule this question would not arise, since the whole amount of the income of the partnership would normally be subject to tax in the State of the partnership. On the other hand, the question would always arise if the special provisions would not be inserted. In that case withholding tax reduction would have to be granted on the basis of the status of each partner for his share of the income. It is an extremely difficult task, particularly if there is a great number of partners being residents of different States, to attribute the income subject to withholding tax to the partners, because the withholding agent does not know the often very complicated and sometimes even abusive arrangements between the partners on the division of profits (and losses). This is the main reason why Germany proposes special provisions on partnerships. As for the last argument put forward in paragraph 45, it is true that the special provision would allow a third State partner to qualify for treaty benefits where the existence of a direct permanent establishment would not, but a strict rule to treat partnership income attributable to a third State partner always

Observations by Germany on paragraph 91 and 92

19.   Germany would prefer an approach under which the partnership as such would be considered as the employer (as under the national law of most OECD member States including Germany even if these States do not tax the partnership as such). Since this employer has to reside somewhere, his residence would have to be determined hypothetically assuming the partnership were liable to tax by reason of one of the criteria mentioned in Article 4. In a case where a partnership established in one Contracting State sends an employee to carry on activities in the other contracting State where it has no permanent establishment, but where one of the partners is resident the difficulties described in paragraph 92 would not arise.

The Netherlands

20.   The conclusions on the treatment of partnerships in the various situations described in the Report are presented as a matter of interpretation of the relevant articles of the Model Convention. We doubt whether these specific conclusions can be said to fully and directly flow from the original intentions underlying the respective articles. We also feel that the conclusions and the reasonings leading to them are not altogether consistent one with the other. In general it seems to us that the wish to provide a certain solution is allowed precedence over the question whether there actually is a legal base for such solution. Furthermore, we are uncertain whether it would be possible under Netherlands domestic law to fully implement the conclusions. Some conclusions might require adaptation of domestic rules (e.g. the participation exemption) that are not governed by a tax treaty. We finally note that the Report does not provide a comprehensive solution for all situations of juridical or economic double taxation or double non-taxation that might arise in the context of partnerships.

21.   According to paragraph 47 of the Report "Member countries may in their bilateral relations develop different solutions to the problems of double taxation which may arise in connection with partnerships". This means that in the absence of such deviating bilateral solutions the conclusions in the Report would automatically prevail. Since bilateral solutions to the issue are still scarce -- we are at this moment in the process of discussing such solutions with some of our major treaty partners and plan to have similar discussions with other treaty partners in the future -- the conclusions in the Report would thus for the time being constitute the main rule. Given the difficulties we have with these conclusions, we would find that an unsatisfactory situation. We therefore prefer it to be up to our own initiative to decide, depending on the

circumstances of the case at hand, whether, and to which extent, the conclusions of the Report are applicable.

22. For similar reasons we prefer also in respect of conflicts of qualification in general to maintain the right to decide ourselves whether the conclusions in the Report may be followed or instead any other solution that appears to be more suitable.

Observations to the proposed paragraphs 2-6 of the Commentary on Article 1

23. In the case of the Netherlands, the conclusions on the application of the Model Convention to partnerships in paragraphs 2-6 and in the Commentaries on other relevant articles are applicable only, and to the extent in which, it is explicitly stated so in a specific double taxation convention, as the result of mutual agreement between competent authorities according to Article 25 or as unilateral policy.

Observation to the proposed paragraphs 32.1-32.7 of the Commentary on Article 23 in respect of conflicts of qualification

24. In the case of the Netherlands, the paragraphs 32.1 to 32.7 regarding conflicts of qualification are applicable only if, and to the extent in which, it is explicitly stated so in a specific double taxation convention, as the result of mutual agreement between competent authorities according to Article 25 or as unilateral policy.

Portugal

25. Portugal, where all partnerships are taxed as such, makes observations on the report since the solutions put forward in that document should be incorporated in special provisions only applicable when included in tax conventions. This is the case, for example, of the treatment of the situation of partners of partnerships — a concept which is considerably fluid given the differences between States — that are fiscally transparent, including the situation where a third State is inserted between the State of source and the State of residence of the partners. The administrative difficulties resulting from some of the solutions put forward should also be noted, as indicated in the report itself in certain cases.

26. Also, the proposed drafting of paragraph 4 of Article 23A could or does raise difficulties with respect to the drafting of paragraph 2 of Article 23A.

Switzerland

27. The rules laid down in proposed paragraph 32 of the Commentary on Article 23 are helpful to avoid double taxation. On the other side they imply the danger that the State of residence becomes dependent on the State of source. If the State of source changes its internal law to enlarge its taxing right the State of residence has to accept it. This could lead to undesirable results. To avoid such results it seems necessary to limit the scope of the rules in paragraphs 32.1-7 to the internal law of both States as it existed in the moment when the Convention was concluded. Problems arising due to changes in the internal law of a State after the conclusion of the Convention should be solved by a revision of the Convention. We would therefore like to insert the following observation to paragraph 32 of the proposed Commentary on Article 23:

> "Switzerland reserves its right not to apply the rules laid down in paragraph 32 in cases where a conflict of qualification results from a modification to the internal law of the State of source subsequent to the conclusion of a Convention."

ANNEX III: LIST OF ENTITIES IN SELECTED COUNTRIES

This annex presents, following a standard format, the main tax treaty characteristics of the various legal forms that a business or investment can take under the domestic laws of the countries that have co-operated to the preparation of this report. It does not cover, however, the case of the individual who has sole ownership or control of a business (i.e. sole proprietorship) or investment. It also does not cover contractual arrangements (i.e. pension funds or investment funds in most countries) which do not create specific new legal forms by themselves but merely use existing legal vehicles (i.e. trusts or companies).

AUSTRALIA

		Partnership	Corporate Limited Partnership[1]	Proprietary Company
1.	Name of entity and common abbreviation			
2.	English translation			
3.	Does the entity file a tax return?	Yes	Yes	Yes
4.	Is tax on the income of the entity assessed on the entity itself?	No	Yes	Yes
5.	Is the tax which is imposed on the income of the entity as it arises a liability of the entity or a liability of the members?	The partners	The entity	The entity
6.	If the tax is paid by the members, how is the income classified for tax purposes?	Retains its fiscal nature	N/A	N/A
7.	Is the rate and type of tax applicable to the entity's income determined on the basis of the members?	Rate determined in relation to each partner	Corporate tax rate is applied	No
8.	Is tax imposed on the recipient when the income of the entity is distributed to its members etc.?	N/A[2]	Yes [3]	Yes
9.	If the answer to 8 is yes, how is that income classified for tax purposes?		Dividend	Dividend
10.	Does your country consider the entity as a "company" for purposes of tax treaties?	No	Yes	Yes
11.	Do you consider the entity a "resident" for purposes of tax treaties?	No	Yes	Yes

APPLICATION OF THE MODEL TAX CONVENTION TO PARTNERSHIPS

AUSTRALIA

1.	Name of entity and common abbreviation	Public Listed Company	Trusts	Corporate Unit Trusts and Public Trading Trusts [4]
2.	English translation			
3.	Does the entity file a tax return?	Yes	Yes	Yes
4.	Is tax on the income of the entity assessed on the entity itself?	Yes	Not generally [5]	Yes
5.	Is the tax which is imposed on the income of the entity as it arises a liability of the entity or a liability of the members?	The entity	The members [6]	The entity
6.	If the tax is paid by the members, how is the income classified for tax purposes?	N/A	Retains its fiscal nature	N/A
7.	Is the rate and type of tax applicable to the entity's income determined on the basis of the members?	No	Rate determined in relation to each beneficiary.	Corporate tax rate is applied
8.	Is tax imposed on the recipient when the income of the entity is distributed to its members etc.?	Yes	N/A	Yes
9.	If the answer to 8 is yes, how is that income classified for tax purposes?	Dividend		Dividend
10.	Does your country consider the entity as a "company" for purposes of tax treaties?	Yes	No	Yes
11.	Do you consider the entity a "resident" for purposes of tax treaties?	Yes	Yes, if trustee is liable to tax	Yes

71

NOTES (AUSTRALIA)

1. Must consist of a general partner, who has unlimited liability for the debts and obligations of the partnership, and one or more limited partners whose liability to the partnership is limited to the amount of money or property which each has contributed.

2. Partnership income is assessed to partners in year of derivation, not year of receipt.

3. Franking credits are available for tax paid directly by the company and for franking credits attached to dividends received. Resident shareholders deriving dividends (including franked dividends) are taxable, but imputation credits apply. A tax liability arises in the hands of the shareholder to the extent that the overall tax burden is higher then the credits attached to any franked dividends received. Franking credits are currently non-refundable and cannot be carried forward or back. For non-residents, dividends are exempt from Australian tax to the extent that they are franked (similar arguments for all entities treated as companies apply.)

4. Must be an eligible unit trust, whose units are traded on the stock exchange. Eligible unit trusts are a type of fixed trusts made up of unit holders having fixed interests in the income and capital of the trust. Common features of these unit trusts are:
   - An independent agent is employed to act as trustee.
   - Units are transferable. The ability to transfer units is often subject to the approval of specified people.
   - Additional units may be issued.
   - Unit holders may attend meetings and vote.

5. Beneficiaries are taxed on income to which they are presently entitled. Trustee will be taxed on any income to which beneficiaries are not entitled or where the beneficiaries are under legal disability or not resident. Non-resident beneficiaries are entitled to a credit for tax paid by trustee.

6. The trustee would also be liable to tax, subject to set off by the beneficiary i.e. reimbursed out of the beneficiary's share of trust property, if the beneficiary is under legal disability.

APPLICATION OF THE MODEL TAX CONVENTION TO PARTNERSHIPS

AUSTRIA

1. Name of entity and common abbreviation	Aktienge-sellschaft (AG)	Gesellschaft mit beschränkter Haftung (GmbH)	Offene Handelsge-sellschaft (OHG)
2. English translation	Company	Limited liability company	General partnership
3. Does the entity file a tax return?	Yes	Yes	No
4. Is tax on the income of the entity assessed on the entity itself?	Yes	Yes	No
5. Is the tax which is imposed on the income of the entity as it arises a liability of the entity or a liability of the members?	The company	The company	The partners
6. If the tax is paid by the members, how is the income classified for tax purposes?	-	-	Fiscal nature is unchanged[2]
7. Is the rate and type of tax applicable to the entity's income determined on the basis of the members?	No	No	-
8. Is tax imposed on the recipient when the income of the entity is distributed to its members etc.?	Yes	Yes	No
9. If the answer to 8 is yes, how is that income classified for tax purposes?	As a dividend	As a dividend	-
10. Does your country consider the entity as a "company" for purposes of tax treaties?	Yes	Yes	No
11. Do you consider the entity a "resident" for purposes of tax treaties?	Yes	Yes	No

AUSTRIA

1.	Name of entity and common abbreviation	Offene Erwerbsge-sellschaft (OEG)	Kommandit gesellschaft (KG)	Kommandit Erwerbsgesellschaft (KEG)
2.	English translation	General partnership type 2[1]	Limited partnership	Limited partnership type 2[5]
3.	Does the entity file a tax return?	No	No	No
4.	Is tax on the income of the entity assessed on the entity itself?	No	No	No
5.	Is the tax which is imposed on the income of the entity as it arises a liability of the entity or a liability of the members?	The partners	The partners	The partners
6.	If the tax is paid by the members, how is the income classified for tax purposes?	Fiscal nature is unchanged[3]	Fiscal nature is unchanged[6]	Fiscal nature is unchanged[7]
7.	Is the rate and type of tax applicable to the entity's income determined on the basis of the members?	-	-	-
8.	Is tax imposed on the recipient when the income of the entity is distributed to its members etc.?	No	No	No
9.	If the answer to 8 is yes, how is that income classified for tax purposes?	-	-	-
10.	Does your country consider the entity as a "company" for purposes of tax treaties?	No	No	No
11.	Do you consider the entity a "resident" for purposes of tax treaties?	No	No	No

APPLICATION OF THE MODEL TAX CONVENTION TO PARTNERSHIPS

AUSTRIA

1.	Name of entity and common abbreviation	Gesellschaft nach bürgerlichem Recht (GesnbR)	Stille Gesellschaft[4]
2.	English translation	Civil law partnership	Sleeping partnership
3.	Does the entity file a tax return?	No	No
4.	Is tax on the income of the entity assessed on the entity itself?	No	No
5.	Is the tax which is imposed on the income of the entity as it arises a liability of the entity or a liability of the members?	The partners	The partners
6.	If the tax is paid by the members, how is the income classified for tax purposes?	Fiscal nature is unchanged[8]	Fiscal nature is unchanged[9]
7.	Is the rate and type of tax applicable to the entity's income determined on the basis of the members?	-	-
8.	Is tax imposed on the recipient when the income of the entity is distributed to its members etc.?	No	No
9.	If the answer to 8 is yes, how is that income classified for tax purposes?	-	-
10.	Does your country consider the entity as a "company" for purposes of tax treaties?	No	No
11.	Do you consider the entity a "resident" for purposes of tax treaties?	No	No

NOTES (AUSTRIA)

1. This form of partnership corresponds to the OHG and was designed for businesses which cannot be carried on in the legal form of an OHG (small - sized businesses, farmers and liberal professions).

2. If, however, part of the activities of the partnership is in the nature of "business income" then the entire partnership income will be reclassified as "business income"

3. See footnote 2.

4. The sleeping partnership is not considered as being a "partnership" under commercial law, because the "sleeping partner" is not made known to third parties. The tax regime for partnerships applies only to those sleeping partnership contracts where the sleeping partner participates not only in the profits but also in the capital gains of the enterprise.

5. This form of partnership corresponds to the KG and was designed for businesses which cannot be carried on in the legal form of a KG (small - sized businesses, farmers and liberal professions).

6. See footnote 2.

7. See footnote 2.

8. See footnote 2.

9. See footnote 2.

APPLICATION OF THE MODEL TAX CONVENTION TO PARTNERSHIPS

BELGIUM

1. Name of entity and common abbreviation	Société anonyme/ Naamloze Vennootschap	Société en commandite par actions/ Commanditaire venootschap op aandelen	Société privée à responsabilité limitée / Besloten venootschap met beperkte aansprakelijkheid
2. English translation	Limited company	Company limited by shares	Limited liability partnership
3. Does the entity file a tax return?	Yes	Yes	Yes
4. Is tax on the income of the entity assessed on the entity itself?	Yes	Yes	Yes
5. Is the tax which is imposed on the income of the entity as it arises a liability of the entity or a liability of the members?	The company	The company	The company
6. If the tax is paid by the members, how is the income classified for tax purposes?	-	-	-
7. Is the rate and type of tax applicable to the entity's income determined on the basis of the members?	No	No	No
8. Is tax imposed on the recipient when the income of the entity is distributed to its members etc.?	Yes	Yes	Yes
9. If the answer to 8 is yes, how is that income classified for tax purposes?	Dividend	Dividend	Dividend
10. Does your country consider the entity as a "company" for purposes of tax treaties?	Yes	Yes	Yes
11. Do you consider the entity a "resident" for purposes of tax treaties?	Yes	Yes	Yes

ISSUES IN INTERNATIONAL TAXATION

BELGIUM

1.	Name of entity and common abbreviation	Société coopérative à responsabilité limitée /Coöperative venootschap met beperkte aansprakelijkheid	Société coopérative à responsabilité illimitée/ Coöperatieve venootschap met onbeperkte aansprakelijkheid
2.	English translation	Co-operative society with limited liability	Co-operative society with unlimited liability
3.	Does the entity file a tax return?	Yes	Yes
4.	Is tax on the income of the entity assessed on the entity itself?	Yes	Yes
5.	Is the tax which is imposed on the income of the entity as it arises a liability of the entity or a liability of the members?	The company	The company
6.	If the tax is paid by the members, how is the income classified for tax purposes?	-	-
7.	Is the rate and type of tax applicable to the entity's income determined on the basis of the members?	No	No
8.	Is tax imposed on the recipient when the income of the entity is distributed to its members etc.?	Yes	Yes
9.	If the answer to 8 is yes, how is that income classified for tax purposes?	Dividend	Dividend
10.	Does your country consider the entity as a "company" for purposes of tax treaties?	Yes	Yes
11.	Do you consider the entity a "resident" for purposes of tax treaties?	Yes	Yes

APPLICATION OF THE MODEL TAX CONVENTION TO PARTNERSHIPS

BELGIUM

1.	Name of entity and common abbreviation	Société en commandite simple/ Gewone commanditaire venootschap	Société en nom collectif/ Vennotschap onder firma
2.	English translation	Limited partnership	General partnership
3.	Does the entity file a tax return?	Yes	Yes
4.	Is tax on the income of the entity assessed on the entity itself?	Yes	Yes
5.	Is the tax which is imposed on the income of the entity as it arises a liability of the entity or a liability of the members?	The company	The company
6.	If the tax is paid by the members, how is the income classified for tax purposes?	-	-
7.	Is the rate and type of tax applicable to the entity's income determined on the basis of the members?	No	No
8.	Is tax imposed on the recipient when the income of the entity is distributed to its members etc.?	Yes	Yes
9.	If the answer to 8 is yes, how is that income classified for tax purposes?	Dividend	Dividend
10.	Does your country consider the entity as a "company" for purposes of tax treaties?	Yes	Yes
11.	Do you consider the entity a "resident" for purposes of tax treaties?	Yes	Yes

ISSUES IN INTERNATIONAL TAXATION

CANADA

		Corporation	Limited Liability Company (LLC)	Partnership (General and Limited)	Trust
1.	Name of entity and common abbreviation				
2.	English translation				
3.	Does the entity file a tax return?	Yes	Yes (considered to be a corporation)	No (an information return may be required)	Yes
4.	Is tax on the income of the entity assessed on the entity itself?	Yes	Yes	No	Yes, to the extent that income of the trust is not paid to beneficiaries[1]
5.	Is the tax which is imposed on the income of the entity as it arises a liability of the entity or a liability of the members?	The entity	The entity	The members	The entity
6.	If the tax is paid by the members, how is the income classified for tax purposes?	-	-	Fiscal nature unchanged	Income from property, with some exceptions in the case of Canadian resident beneficiaries[2]
7.	Is the rate and type of tax applicable to the entity's income determined on the basis of the members?	No	No	Yes	No, to the extent taxed at the level of the trust
8.	Is tax imposed on the recipient when the income of the entity is distributed to its members etc.?	Yes, except certain dividends[3]	Yes, except certain dividends[4]	No	See 6 above
9.	If the answer to 8 is yes, how is that income classified for tax purposes?	Dividend	Dividend	-	Trust income or retains its nature (see 6 above)
10.	Does your country consider the entity as a "company" for purposes of tax treaties?	Yes	Yes	No	No
11.	Do you consider the entity a "resident" for purposes of tax treaties?	Yes	Yes	No	Yes

APPLICATION OF THE MODEL TAX CONVENTION TO PARTNERSHIPS

NOTES (CANADA)

1. A trust which is resident in Canada is entitled to a deduction from its income for a taxation year to the extent it is paid or payable to a beneficiary in the year. In this way the trust is not taxed on such income.

2. For Canadian resident beneficiaries certain income (e.g. dividends, capital gains) retains its source and character for the purpose of calculating taxable income and tax payable of the beneficiary.

3. Dividends received by a Canadian corporation from another are tax free (by way of deduction from income), except certain dividends received by Canadian private corporations.

4. See previous footnote.

CZECH REPUBLIC

1. Name of entity and common abbreviation	Akciová společnost, a.s.	Společnost s ručením omezeným, s.r.o.	Komanditní společnost, k.s.[1]	Veřejná obchodní společnost, v.o.s.
2. English translation	Joint-stock company	Limited liability company	Limited partnership	General partnership
3. Does the entity file a tax return?	Yes	Yes	Yes	No
4. Is tax on the income of the entity assessed on the entity itself?	Yes	Yes	Yes	-
5. Is the tax which is imposed on the income of the entity as it arises a liability of the entity or a liability of the members?	The company	The company	Both	The partners
6. If the tax is paid by the members, how is the income classified for tax purposes?	-	-	Business income	Business income
7. Is the rate and type of tax applicable to the entity's income determined on the basis of the members?	No	No	Yes	Yes
8. Is tax imposed on the recipient when the income of the entity is distributed to its members etc.?	Yes (25% withholding)	Yes (25% withholding)	Yes	-
9. If the answer to 8 is yes, how is that income classified for tax purposes?	Dividends	Shares	Shares	-
10. Does your country consider the entity as a "company" for purposes of tax treaties?	Yes	Yes	Yes	Yes
11. Do you consider the entity a "resident" for purposes of tax treaties?	Yes	Yes	Yes	No

APPLICATION OF THE MODEL TAX CONVENTION TO PARTNERSHIPS

NOTES (CZECH REPUBLIC)

1. A limited partnership is considered, in accordance with the Czech Commercial Law, as a legal entity in the Czech Republic. The tax base is calculated under the same rules as for a joint stock company and a limited liability company. However, from the tax point of view, the limited partnership is a person the tax base of which is divided among its general partners and limited partners. The income which corresponds to the income of the general partners is taxed as business income in the hands of these partners. The general partner has to include this income in his income tax return. The income which corresponds to the income of the limited partners is taxed as a business income of a company (taxation of a legal person - the share of the general partners is deducted form the tax base of the company); distributions made to the limited partners from the after-tax profits of the company are taxed in their hands (at 25 %).

2. A general partnership is also considered, in accordance with the Czech Commercial Law, as a legal entity in the Czech Republic. From the tax point of view, however, the income of the general partnership is divided among the partners according to their respective share (transparency). The income of the partnership is therefore taxable in the hands of the partners. Income such as dividends and interest (when withholding tax is applicable) constitutes an exception to this rule. In that respect, a general partnership is a taxpayer in the Czech Republic only to a very limited extent.

DENMARK

1.	Name of entity and common abbreviation	Skattesinteres sentskab[1]	Interessentskab I/S Partrederi[2]	Kommandit-Selskab K/S
2.	English translation	General partnership	General partnership, owned shipping firm	Limited partnership
3.	Does the entity file a tax return?	No	No	No
4.	Is tax on the income of the entity assessed on the entity itself?	No	No	No
5.	Is the tax which is imposed on the income of the entity as it arises a liability of the entity or a liability of the members?	The partners	The partners	The partners
6.	If the tax is paid by the members, how is the income classified for tax purposes?	Business income	Capital income[3]	Business income
7.	Is the rate and type of tax applicable to the entity's income determined on the basis of the members?	-	-	-
8.	Is tax imposed on the recipient when the income of the entity is distributed to its members etc.?	No	No	No
9.	If the answer to 8 is yes, how is that income classified for tax purposes?	-	-	-
10.	Does your country consider the entity as a "company" for purposes of tax treaties?	No	No	No
11.	Do you consider the entity a "resident" for purposes of tax treaties?	No	No	No

APPLICATION OF THE MODEL TAX CONVENTION TO PARTNERSHIPS

DENMARK

1.	Name of entity and common abbreviation	Udloddende investerings-forening[4]	Andelsforening[5]	Institutioner[9]
2.	English translation	Distributing investment fund	Co-operative association	Association
3.	Does the entity file a tax return?	No	Yes[6]	Yes[10]
4.	Is tax on the income of the entity assessed on the entity itself?	No	Yes[7]	Yes
5.	Is the tax which is imposed on the income of the entity as it arises a liability of the entity or a liability of the members?	The members	The association	The association
6.	If the tax is paid by the members, how is the income classified for tax purposes?	Fiscal nature is unchanged	Business income	Business income
7.	Is the rate and type of tax applicable to the entity's income determined on the basis of the members?		No[8]	No
8.	Is tax imposed on the recipient when the income of the entity is distributed to its members etc.?	Yes	Yes	Yes
9.	If the answer to 8 is yes, how is that income classified for tax purposes?	Fiscal nature is unchanged	Dividends	Dividends or ordinary income[11]
10.	Does your country consider the entity as a "company" for purposes of tax treaties?	Yes	Yes	Yes
11.	Do you consider the entity a "resident" for purposes of tax treaties?	Yes	Yes	Yes

NOTES (DENMARK)

1. A general partnership is also called a limited liability company. The characteristic of such a company is that there are more than 10 partners and that the partners do not take an active part in the company's activity.

2. Unlike the partners in a general partnership, the part owners of an owned shipping firm are liable pro rata in accordance with the Maritime Code.

3. There is only limited access to loss carry forward

4. Funds which annually distribute almost all profits

5. The association must buy, produce or sell commercial goods for the use of members' commercial undertakings and distribute profits in proportion to the turnover of individual members. There must be at least 10 members and sales to non-members must not exceed 25% of total sales.

6. Only income from commercial activity must be returned.

7. Income is assumed to be 4% of the association's capital and this is taxed at 14.3%.

8. But taxation of the association is affected by the value of transactions with non-members, if such transactions consistently exceed 25% of sales the association will be taxed as a normal company.

9. The association is liable to pay tax only on income from commercial activity. Profits earned by internal sale, i.e. by delivery to the members are not earned by commercial activity.

10. See footnote 6.

11. Dividends where members participate in the co-operative share capital, otherwise ordinary income.

APPLICATION OF THE MODEL TAX CONVENTION TO PARTNERSHIPS

FINLAND

1.	Name of entity and common abbreviation	Avoin yhtiö / Öppet bolag	Kommandiitiyhtiö (Ky)/ Kommanditbolag (Kb)	Osakeyhtiö (Oy) /Aktiebolag (Ab)
2.	English translation	General partnership	Limited partnership	Limited company
3.	Does the entity file a tax return?	Yes	Yes	Yes
4.	Is tax on the income of the entity assessed on the entity itself?[1]	No	No	Yes
5.	Is the tax which is imposed on the income of the entity as it arises a liability of the entity or a liability of the members?[2]	Each partner	Each partner	The company
6.	If the tax is paid by the members, how is the income classified for tax purposes?[3]	Investment income	Investment income	-
7.	Is the rate and type of tax applicable to the entity's income determined on the basis of the members?	Yes	Yes	-
8.	Is tax imposed on the recipient when the income of the entity is distributed to its members etc.?	No	No	Yes
9.	If the answer to 8 is yes, how is that income classified for tax purposes?	-	-	Dividends
10.	Does your country consider the entity as a "company" for purposes of tax treaties?	No	No	Yes
11.	Do you consider the entity a "resident" for purposes of tax treaties?	No	No	Yes

NOTES (FINLAND)

1. The total taxable income is computed at the level of the partnership. The tax, however, is assessed on each partner separately (i.e. tax demand notes are issued on each partner) on the basis of his share of the partnership income. The partner is responsible for his own tax.

2. See previous footnote.

3. The income of individuals is categorised either as investment income or as earned income. Investment income is defined as the proceeds from capital, gains from the disposal of assets (capital gains) and other income yielded by assets. The following items of income are examples of investment income: interest and rental income, dividends from companies listed on the stock exchange, income from forestry (with exceptions) and income from patents or copyrights (on certain conditions). Earned income is defined as any income other than investment income. Investment income includes, in addition to the items listed above, the investment income *share* of certain types of "mixed" income, such as dividends from companies *not* listed on a stock exchange, profits from business, income from agriculture and income from partnerships. Corporate income and the investment income of individuals are taxed at the same flat rate (28 per cent).

APPLICATION OF THE MODEL TAX CONVENTION TO PARTNERSHIPS

FRANCE

1.	Name of entity and common abbreviation	Société anonyme (S.A.)	Société à responsabilité limitée (S.A.R.L.)[1]	Société en nom collectif (S.N.C.)[7]
2.	English translation	Company limited by shares	Limited liability company	General partnership
3.	Does the entity file a tax return?	Yes	Yes	Yes
4.	Is tax on the income of the entity assessed on the entity itself?	Yes	Yes	No
5.	Is the tax which is imposed on the income of the entity as it arises a liability of the entity or a liability of the members?	Of the entity	Of the entity	Of the partners
6.	If the tax is paid by the members, how is the income classified for tax purposes?	-	-	The answer depends on the characteristics of the partners or on the nature of the partnership's activity[2]
7.	Is the rate and type of tax applicable to the entity's income determined on the basis of the members?	-	-	Yes
8.	Is tax imposed on the recipient when the income of the entity is distributed to its members etc.?	Yes	Yes	No
9.	If the answer to 8 is yes, how is that income classified for tax purposes?	Dividends	Dividends	-
10.	Does your country consider the entity as a "company" for purposes of tax treaties?	Yes	Yes	Yes
11.	Do you consider the entity a "resident" for purposes of tax treaties?	Yes	Yes	Yes

FRANCE

1.	Name of entity and common abbreviation	Société en commandite simple (S.C.S.)[3 & 7]	Société en commandite par actions (S.C.A.)	Groupement d'intérêt économique (G.I.E.)[7]
2.	English translation	Limited partnership	Limited partnership with share capital	Economic interest grouping
3.	Does the entity file a tax return?	Yes	Yes	Yes
4.	Is tax on the income of the entity assessed on the entity itself?	Yes/No[3]	Yes	No
5.	Is the tax which is imposed on the income of the entity as it arises a liability of the entity or a liability of the members?	Of the entity and of the partners[4]	Of the entity	Of the partners
6.	If the tax is paid by the members, how is the income classified for tax purposes?	The answer depends on the characteristics of the partners or on the nature of the partnership's activity[5]	-	The answer depends on the characteristics of the partners or on the nature of the partnership's activity[5]
7.	Is the rate and type of tax applicable to the entity's income determined on the basis of the members?	Yes/No[6]	No	Yes
8.	Is tax imposed on the recipient when the income of the entity is distributed to its members etc.?	Yes/No[3]	Yes	No
9.	If the answer to 8 is yes, how is that income classified for tax purposes?	Dividends in the hands of the limited partners	Dividends	-
10.	Does your country consider the entity as a "company" for purposes of tax treaties?	Yes	Yes	Yes
11.	Do you consider the entity a "resident" for purposes of tax treaties?	Yes	Yes	Yes

APPLICATION OF THE MODEL TAX CONVENTION TO PARTNERSHIPS

FRANCE

1.	Name of entity and common abbreviation	Société civile[7]	Société en participation[7 & 8]
2.	English translation	Civil partnership	Undeclared partnership
3.	Does the entity file a tax return?	Yes	Yes
4.	Is tax on the income of the entity assessed on the entity itself?	No	No
5.	Is the tax which is imposed on the income of the entity as it arises a liability of the entity or a liability of the members?	Of the partners	Of the partners
6.	If the tax is paid by the members, how is the income classified for tax purposes?	The answer depends on the characteristics of the partners or on the nature of the partnership's activity[5]	The answer depends on the characteristics of the partners or on the nature of the partnership's activity[5]
7.	Is the rate and type of tax applicable to the entity's income determined on the basis of the members?	Yes	Yes
8.	Is tax imposed on the recipient when the income of the entity is distributed to its members etc.?	No	No
9.	If the answer to 8 is yes, how is that income classified for tax purposes?	-	-
10.	Does your country consider the entity as a "company" for purposes of tax treaties?	Yes	Yes
11.	Do you consider the entity a "resident" for purposes of tax treaties?	Yes	Yes

NOTES (FRANCE)

1. With the exception of limited liability companies set up by members of the same family, which can opt for the tax regime applicable to partnerships. If so, the regime is equivalent to that applicable to a general partnership.

2. The methods used to calculate taxable profits differ according to the quality of the members of the partnership:
    a) the share in profits corresponding to the rights of partners which are legal entities liable to corporation tax or individual farmers who come under a real business profits system (BIC) or a farm profits system (BA) is calculated in accordance with the relevant rules regarding corporation tax, business profits or farm profits (Article 238 bis K I of the general tax code);
    b) the shares in profits accruing to other companies are calculated and taxed on the basis of the nature of the activity and the amount of earnings of the company or partnership (Article 238 bis K II of the general tax code).

3. Unlike a general partnership, in which all the members have unlimited liability, a limited partnership is a company in which at least one of the partners is held indefinitely liable for the company's debts. The share of profits accruing to that partner or those partners is taxable according to the rules of French tax law applying to partnerships (the same system as for a general partnership). By contrast, the share of profits accruing to the sleeping partners is taxed in France according to the rules applying to joint-stock companies (corporation tax in the name of the company and taxation as dividends of the income distributed by the company to its general partners).

4. Of the company where the share of profits accruing to sleeping partners is concerned; of the partners where the share of profits accruing to general partners is concerned.

5. See footnote 2.

6. Yes, where the profits corresponding to general partners' earnings entitlements are concerned; no, where the share in profits accruing to sleeping partners is concerned.

7. With the exception of civil partnerships, general partnerships, undeclared partnerships, economic interest groupings, and limited partnerships with respect to the share of profits accruing to general partners, which, if they have elected to be liable to corporation tax, are subjected to the same tax regime as that applying to limited companies.

8. In proportion to the share of profits accruing to their members who are indefinitely liable and whose names and addresses have been given to the authorities.

APPLICATION OF THE MODEL TAX CONVENTION TO PARTNERSHIPS

GERMANY

1.	Name of entity and common abbreviation	Aktien gesellschaft (AG)	Gesellschaft mit beschrankter Haftung (GmbH)	Kommanditge-sellschaft auf Aktien (KGaA)
2.	English translation	Limited liability company	Limited liability company	Partnership limited by shares
3.	Does the entity file a tax return?	Yes	Yes	Yes
4.	Is tax on the income of the entity assessed on the entity itself?	Yes	Yes	Yes
5.	Is the tax which is imposed on the income of the entity as it arises a liability of the entity or a liability of the members?	The company	The company	The partners / company[1]
6.	If the tax is paid by the members, how is the income classified for tax purposes?	-	-	Business income
7.	Is the rate and type of tax applicable to the entity's income determined on the basis of the members?			
8.	Is tax imposed on the recipient when the income of the entity is distributed to its members etc.?	Yes	Yes	Yes[2]
9.	If the answer to 8 is yes, how is that income classified for tax purposes?	Dividends	Dividends	Dividends
10.	Does your country consider the entity as a "company" for purposes of tax treaties?	Yes	Yes	Yes
11.	Do you consider the entity a "resident" for purposes of tax treaties?	Yes	Yes	Yes[3]

ISSUES IN INTERNATIONAL TAXATION

GERMANY

1. Name of entity and common abbreviation	Gesellschaft bürgerlichen Rechts (GbR)	Offene Handelsge-sellschaft (OHG)	Kommandit Gesellschaft (KG)	Stille Gesellschaft
2. English translation	Civil law partnership	General partnership	Limited partnership	Silent partnership
3. Does the entity file a tax return?	No	No	No	No
4. Is tax on the income of the entity assessed on the entity itself?	No	No	No	No
5. Is the tax which is imposed on the income of the entity as it arises a liability of the entity or a liability of the members?	The partners	The partners	The partners	The partners
6. If the tax is paid by the members, how is the income classified for tax purposes?	Dependent upon nature of activity[4]	Business income	Business income	Investment income[5]
7. Is the rate and type of tax applicable to the entity's income determined on the basis of the members?				
8. Is tax imposed on the recipient when the income of the entity is distributed to its members etc.?	No	No	No	No
9. If the answer to 8 is yes, how is that income classified for tax purposes?	-	-	-	-
10. Does your country consider the entity as a "company" for purposes of tax treaties?	No	No	No	No
11. Do you consider the entity a "resident" for purposes of tax treaties?	No[6]	No[7]	No[8]	No

94

APPLICATION OF THE MODEL TAX CONVENTION TO PARTNERSHIPS

NOTES (GERMANY)

1. The share of the general partner is deducted from the tax base of the company. The general partner must include this share in his income tax return.
2. No, in the case of the general partner.
3. Unclear as far as the general partner is concerned.
4. Income from agriculture or forestry, from independent services, business income or investment income.
5. The active partner earns business income.
6. Under specific provisions of conventions the entity may be deemed to be a resident for the purposes of the convention.
7. See footnote 6.
8. See footnote 6

HUNGARY

1.	Name of entity and common abbreviation	Korlátolt felelősségü társaság (Kft)	Részvény-társaság (Rt.)	Egyesülés
2.	English translation	Limited liability company	Company limited by shares	Professional association
3.	Does the entity file a tax return?	Yes	Yes	Yes
4.	Is tax on the income of the entity assessed on the entity itself?	Yes	Yes	Yes
5.	Is the tax which is imposed on the income of the entity as it arises a liability of the entity or a liability of the members?	The company	The company	The company
6.	If the tax is paid by the members, how is the income classified for tax purposes?	-	-	-
7.	Is the rate and type of tax applicable to the entity's income determined on the basis of the members?	-	-	-
8.	Is tax imposed on the recipient when the income of the entity is distributed to its members etc.?	Yes	Yes	Yes
9.	If the answer to 8 is yes, how is that income classified for tax purposes?	Dividend	Dividend	Dividend
10.	Does your country consider the entity as a "company" for purposes of tax treaties?	Yes	Yes	Yes
11.	Do you consider the entity a "resident" for purposes of tax treaties?	Yes	Yes	Yes

APPLICATION OF THE MODEL TAX CONVENTION TO PARTNERSHIPS

HUNGARY

1. Name of entity and common abbreviation	Közkereseti társaság (Kkt)	Betéti társaság (Bt.)	Közös vállalat	Szövetkezet
2. English translation	Unlimited partnership	Limited partnership	Joint enterprises	Co-operative
3. Does the entity file a tax return?	Yes	Yes	Yes	Yes
4. Is tax on the income of the entity assessed on the entity itself?	Yes	Yes	Yes	Yes
5. Is the tax which is imposed on the income of the entity as it arises a liability of the entity or a liability of the members?	The company	The company	The company	The company
6. If the tax is paid by the members, how is the income classified for tax purposes?	-	-	-	-
7. Is the rate and type of tax applicable to the entity's income determined on the basis of the members?	-	-	-	-
8. Is tax imposed on the recipient when the income of the entity is distributed to its members etc.?	Yes	Yes	Yes	Yes
9. If the answer to 8 is yes, how is that income classified for tax purposes?	Dividend	Dividend	Dividend	Dividend
10. Does your country consider the entity as a "company" for purposes of tax treaties?	Yes	Yes	Yes	Yes
11. Do you consider the entity a "resident" for purposes of tax treaties?	Yes	Yes	Yes	Yes

ISSUES IN INTERNATIONAL TAXATION

ICELAND

1. Name of entity and common abbreviation	Hlutafélag	Sameignarfélag skráð sem sjálfstaeður skattaðili	Sameignarfélag
2. English translation	Public limited liability company	Partnership registered as a taxable entity	Partnership
3. Does the entity file a tax return?	Yes	Yes	No
4. Is tax on the income of the entity assessed on the entity itself?	Yes	Yes	No
5. Is the tax which is imposed on the income of the entity as it arises a liability of the entity or a liability of the members?	The company	The company	The partners
6. If the tax is paid by the members, how is the income classified for tax purposes?	-	-	Business income
7. Is the rate and type of tax applicable to the entity's income determined on the basis of the members?	No	No	Yes
8. Is tax imposed on the recipient when the income of the entity is distributed to its members etc.?	Yes	No	No
9. If the answer to 8 is yes, how is that income classified for tax purposes?	Dividends	-	-
10. Does your country consider the entity as a "company" for purposes of tax treaties?	Yes	Yes	No
11. Do you consider the entity a "resident" for purposes of tax treaties?	Yes	Yes	No

APPLICATION OF THE MODEL TAX CONVENTION TO PARTNERSHIPS

JAPAN

1.	Name of entity and common abbreviation	Kabushiki-kaisha[1]	Yugen-kaisha[2]	Gomei-kaisha[3]	Goshi-kaisha[4]
2.	English translation	Joint Stock Company	Limited Liability Company	•	•
3.	Does the entity file a tax return?	Yes	Yes	Yes	Yes
4.	Is tax on the income of the entity assessed on the entity itself?	Yes	Yes	Yes	Yes
5.	Is the tax which is imposed on the income of the entity as it arises a liability of the entity or a liability of the members?	The entity	The entity	The entity	The entity
6.	If the tax is paid by the members, how is the income classified for tax purposes?	-	-	-	-
7.	Is the rate and type of tax applicable to the entity's income determined on the basis of the members?	No	No	No	No
8.	Is tax imposed on the recipient when the income of the entity is distributed to its members etc.?	Yes	Yes	Yes	Yes
9.	If the answer to 8 is yes, how is that income classified for tax purposes?	Dividends	Dividends	Dividends	Dividends
10.	Does your country consider the entity as a "company" for purposes of tax treaties?	Yes	Yes	Yes	Yes
11.	Do you consider the entity a "resident" for purposes of tax treaties?	Yes	Yes	Yes	Yes

ISSUES IN INTERNATIONAL TAXATION

JAPAN

1.	Name of entity and common abbreviation	Kumiai[5]	Tokumei Kumiai[6]	Kyodo-Kumiai[7]	Jinkaku-naki-shadan[8]
2.	English translation	-		Cooperative Association	-
3.	Does the entity file a tax return?	No	No	Yes	Yes
4.	Is tax on the income of the entity assessed on the entity itself?	No	No	Yes	Yes
5.	Is the tax which is imposed on the income of the entity as it arises a liability of the entity or a liability of the members?	The members	The members	The entity	The entity
6.	If the tax is paid by the members, how is the income classified for tax purposes?	Fiscal nature is unchanged	Fiscal nature is unchanged[9]	-	-
7.	Is the rate and type of tax applicable to the entity's income determined on the basis of the members?	-		-	-
8.	Is tax imposed on the recipient when the income of the entity is distributed to its members etc.?	No	Yes Withholding at the rate of 20%[10]	Yes	Yes
9.	If the answer to 8 is yes, how is that income classified for tax purposes?		Fiscal nature is unchanged[11]	Dividends	Dividends
10.	Does your country consider the entity as a "company" for purposes of tax treaties?	No	No	Yes	Yes
11.	Do you consider the entity a "resident" for purposes of tax treaties?	No	No	Yes	Yes

100

APPLICATION OF THE MODEL TAX CONVENTION TO PARTNERSHIPS

NOTES (JAPAN)

1. An ordinary corporation, organized under the Commercial Code. All shareholders have limited liability.

2. Commonly used by small businesses and organized under the Limited Liability Company Law. All members have limited liability.

3. Members have unlimited liability for the debts of the entity. It is a legal entity organized under the Commercial Code and subject to corporate taxation.

4. There must be at least one member with unlimited liability and one member with limited liability. A limited liability member may not participate in the management. It is a legal entity organized under the Commercial Code and subject to corporate taxation.

5. A joint contract, under the Civil Code, and not a separate legal entity itself.

6. Formed under the Commercial Code and completely different from "*Kumiai*". It might be compared to the German "stille gesellshaft", one distinctive feature of this type of contract is that only the entrepreneur is recognized as an entity that undertakes its business.

7. Incorporated by special legislation. These entities are listed in Schedule III of the Corporation Tax Law and subject to corporate taxation at a lower rate.

8. Might be translated as "non-juridical organisation": an unincorporated organisation which has designated managers or representatives. Subject to corporate taxation only when it undertakes profit-making activities prescribed under the law.

9. The entrepreneur reports all profits under the *Tokumei-kumiai*. When the entrepreneur distributes profits to the investors, the distribution is subject to withholding tax unless the number of investors is less than ten. If the investors are non-resident, the income is classified as income arising from property located in Japan.

10. See previous footnote.

11. See previous footnote.

LUXEMBOURG

		Société anonyme (S.A.)	Société à responsabilité limitée (SARL)	Société en commandite simple (SECS)	Société en commandite par actions (SECA)
1.	Name of entity and common abbreviation	Société anonyme (S.A.)	Société à responsabilité limitée (SARL)	Société en commandite simple (SECS)	Société en commandite par actions (SECA)
2.	English translation	Company limited by shares	Limited liability company	Limited partnership	Limited partnership with share capital
3.	Does the entity file a tax return?	Yes	Yes	Yes	Yes
4.	Is tax on the income of the entity assessed on the entity itself?	Yes	Yes	No	Yes
5.	Is the tax which is imposed on the income of the entity as it arises a liability of the entity or a liability of the members?	The company	The company	The partners	The partners / the company[1]
6.	If the tax is paid by the members, how is the income classified for tax purposes?	-	-	Business profits	Business profits
7.	Is the rate and type of tax applicable to the entity's income determined on the basis of the members?				
8.	Is tax imposed on the recipient when the income of the entity is distributed to its members etc.?	Yes	Yes	No	Yes[2]
9.	If the answer to 8 is yes, how is that income classified for tax purposes?	As a dividend	As a dividend		As a dividend
10.	Does your country consider the entity as a "company" for purposes of tax treaties?	Yes	Yes	No	Yes
11.	Do you consider the entity a "resident" for purposes of tax treaties?	Yes	Yes	No	Yes

APPLICATION OF THE MODEL TAX CONVENTION TO PARTNERSHIPS

LUXEMBOURG

1. Name of entity and common abbreviation	Société en nom collectif (SENC)	Société coopérative	Société civile	Association en participation
2. English translation	General partnership	Co-operative	Civil partnership	Undeclared partnership
3. Does the entity file a tax return?	Yes	Yes	Yes	No
4. Is tax on the income of the entity assessed on the entity itself?	No	Yes	No	No
5. Is the tax which is imposed on the income of the entity as it arises a liability of the entity or a liability of the members?	The partners	The entity	The partners	The partners
6. If the tax is paid by the members, how is the income classified for tax purposes?	Business profits		Depends on the nature of the activity[3]	Investment income[4]
7. Is the rate and type of tax applicable to the entity's income determined on the basis of the members?				
8. Is tax imposed on the recipient when the income of the entity is distributed to its members etc.?	No	Yes	No	No
9. If the answer to 8 is yes, how is that income classified for tax purposes?		As a dividend		
10. Does your country consider the entity as a "company" for purposes of tax treaties?	No	Yes	No	No
11. Do you consider the entity a "resident" for purposes of tax treaties?	No	Yes	No	No

NOTES (LUXEMBOURG)

1. The share of the general partner is deducted from the tax base of the partnership. The general partner must report that share in his income tax return.
2. No, in the case of the general partner.
3. Income from farming or forestry, rents, income from independent services, business profits or investment income.
4. Income of the active partner is considered to be business profits.

APPLICATION OF THE MODEL TAX CONVENTION TO PARTNERSHIPS

MEXICO

1.	Name of entity and common abbreviation	Asosiación en Participación[1] (A en P)
2.	English translation	
3.	Does the entity file a tax return?	Yes
4.	Is tax on the income of the entity assessed on the entity itself?	Yes
5.	Is the tax which is imposed on the income of the entity as it arises a liability of the entity or a liability of the members?	The entity[2]
6.	If the tax is paid by the members, how is the income classified for tax purposes?	-
7.	Is the rate and type of tax applicable to the entity's income determined on the basis of the members?	No
8.	Is tax imposed on the recipient when the income of the entity is distributed to its members etc.?	Yes
9.	If the answer to 8 is yes, how is that income classified for tax purposes?	Dividend
10.	Does your country consider the entity as a "company" for purposes of tax treaties?	Yes[3]
11.	Do you consider the entity a "resident" for purposes of tax treaties?	Yes

105

NOTES (MEXICO)

1. According to Mexican Civil Law, the A en P is a non-corporate entity, since its legal nature is that of a contract.

2. The tax shall be paid by one of the members on behalf of the entity with respect to its total income which is considered as business income. If such member does not pay the tax, the other members are jointly liable for the tax.

3. Although the A en P is not considered a company under Mexican Civil Law, it is taxed as a corporation for tax purposes, as of 1999.

APPLICATION OF THE MODEL TAX CONVENTION TO PARTNERSHIPS

NETHERLANDS

1.	Name of entity and common abbreviation	Vennootschap onder firma (V.O.F.)	Commanditaire vennootschap (C.V.)	Open Commanditaire vennootschap (open C.V.)
2.	English translation	General partnership	Limited partnership	"Open" limited partnership – free transferability of shares
3.	Does the entity file a tax return?	No	No	Yes – only for income attributed to the limited members (partners)
4.	Is tax on the income of the entity assessed on the entity itself?	No	No	As for 3.
5.	Is the tax which is imposed on the income of the entity as it arises a liability of the entity or a liability of the members?	The members	The members	The entity
6.	If the tax is paid by the members, how is the income classified for tax purposes?	Fiscal nature unchanged	Fiscal nature unchanged	Fiscal nature unchanged
7.	Is the rate and type of tax applicable to the entity's income determined on the basis of the members?	Rate determined in relation to each member	Rate determined in relation to each member	Rate determined in relation to each general member (partner)
8.	Is tax imposed on the recipient when the income of the entity is distributed to its members etc.?	No	No	Only if the recipient is a limited member (partner)
9.	If the answer to 8 is yes, how is that income classified for tax purposes?	-	-	Dividend
10.	Does your country consider the entity as a "company" for purposes of tax treaties?	No	No	Yes
11.	Do you consider the entity a "resident" for purposes of tax treaties?	No	No	Yes

NETHERLANDS

1.	Name of entity and common abbreviation	Naamloze vennootschap (N.V.)	Besloten vennootschap (B.V.)	Maatschap
2.	English translation	Joint stock company	Limited company	Partnership
3.	Does the entity file a tax return?	Yes	Yes	No
4.	Is tax on the income of the entity assessed on the entity itself?	Yes	Yes	No
5.	Is the tax which is imposed on the income of the entity as it arises a liability of the entity or a liability of the members?	The entity	The entity	The members
6.	If the tax is paid by the members, how is the income classified for tax purposes?	-	-	Fiscal nature unchanged
7.	Is the rate and type of tax applicable to the entity's income determined on the basis of the members?	No, same for all income	No, same for all income	Yes, rate determined in relation to each member
8.	Is tax imposed on the recipient when the income of the entity is distributed to its members etc.?	Yes	Yes	No
9.	If the answer to 8 is yes, how is that income classified for tax purposes?	Dividend	Dividend	-
10.	Does your country consider the entity as a "company" for purposes of tax treaties?	Yes	Yes	No
11.	Do you consider the entity a "resident" for purposes of tax treaties?	Yes	Yes	No

APPLICATION OF THE MODEL TAX CONVENTION TO PARTNERSHIPS

NEW ZEALAND

1.	Name of entity and common abbreviation	Partnerships (ordinary)	Special Partnerships[1]	Qualifying Companies[2]
2.	English translation	-	-	-
3.	Does the entity file a tax return?	Yes	Yes	Yes
4.	Is tax on the income of the entity assessed on the entity itself?	No	No	Yes
5.	Is the tax which is imposed on the income of the entity as it arises a liability of the entity or a liability of the members?	Partners	Partners	Company pays the tax in the first instance, but shareholders liable if Company defaults
6.	If the tax is paid by the members, how is the income classified for tax purposes?	Retains its original character	Retains its original character	-
7.	Is the rate and type of tax applicable to the entity's income determined on the basis of the members?	Yes	Yes	No
8.	Is tax imposed on the recipient when the income of the entity is distributed to its members etc.?	No	No	No
9.	If the answer to 8 is yes, how is that income classified for tax purposes?	-	-	-
10.	Does your country consider the entity as a "company" for purposes of tax treaties?	No	No	Yes
11.	Do you consider the entity a "resident" for purposes of tax treaties?	No	No	Yes

NOTES (NEW ZEALAND)

1. Some of the partners of Special Partnerships have limited liability status.
2. Qualifying Companies may not earn more than NZ$10,000 otherwise status reverts to that of an ordinary company

APPLICATION OF THE MODEL TAX CONVENTION TO PARTNERSHIPS

NORWAY

1.	Name of entity and common abbreviation	Ansvarlig selskap	Kommandit selskap	Indre selskap	Aksjeselskap
2.	English translation	General partnership[1]	Limited partnership[2]	Silent partnership[3]	Limited liability company
3.	Does the entity file a tax return?	No	No	No	Yes
4.	Is tax on the income of the entity assessed on the entity itself?	No	No	No	Yes
5.	Is the tax which is imposed on the income of the entity as it arises a liability of the entity or a liability of the members?	The partners	The partners	The partners	The company
6.	If the tax is paid by the members, how is the income classified for tax purposes?	Business income[4]	Business income	Business income	-
7.	Is the rate and type of tax applicable to the entity's income determined on the basis of the members?				
8.	Is tax imposed on the recipient when the income of the entity is distributed to its members etc.?	No	No	No	Yes
9.	If the answer to 8 is yes, how is that income classified for tax purposes?	-	-	-	Dividends
10.	Does your country consider the entity as a "company" for purposes of tax treaties?	No	No	No	Yes
11.	Do you consider the entity a "resident" for purposes of tax treaties?	No	No	No	Yes

NOTES (NORWAY)

1. A General partnership is an enterprise where the partners have an unlimited personal responsibility for the aggregate liabilities of the enterprise, jointly, or partly if the parts put together constitute the whole of the liabilities of the enterprise and the enterprise acts as such towards third parties. For taxation purposes there are no differences.

2. A limited partnership is an enterprise where at least one of the partners has an unlimited responsibility for the liabilities of the enterprise and there is at least one partner who has a limited responsibility for a stated amount of the liabilities of the enterprise unless that partner is a silent partner.

3. Silent partnership is an enterprise which does not act as such towards third parties. The partners may have either limited or unlimited responsibility.

4. The income of the partnership will be regarded as business income. In relation to partners resident abroad, the result will depend upon whether the partners have a permanent establishment or not. If they have a p.e., the income will be regarded as business income. If the partners receive only passive income (no p.e.), the nature of the income (e.g. dividends, interest or royalty) is considered and the relevant article of the convention is applied.

APPLICATION OF THE MODEL TAX CONVENTION TO PARTNERSHIPS

POLAND

1.	Name of entity and common abbreviation	Spólka komadytowa	Spólka jawna	Spólka prawa cywolnego (s.c)
2.	English translation	Limited partnership	Registered partnership	Civil law partnership
3.	Does the entity file a tax return?	No	No	No
4.	Is tax on the income of the entity assessed on the entity itself?	No	No	No
5.	Is the tax which is imposed on the income of the entity as it arises a liability of the entity or a liability of the members?	The partners	The partners	The partners
6.	If the tax is paid by the members, how is the income classified for tax purposes?	Fiscal nature is unchanged	Fiscal nature is unchanged	Fiscal nature is unchanged
7.	Is the rate and type of tax applicable to the entity's income determined on the basis of the members?	-	-	-
8.	Is tax imposed on the recipient when the income of the entity is distributed to its members etc.?	No	No	No
9.	If the answer to 8 is yes, how is that income classified for tax purposes?	-	-	-
10.	Does your country consider the entity as a "company" for purposes of tax treaties?	No	No	No
11.	Do you consider the entity a "resident" for purposes of tax treaties?	No	No	No

SLOVAK REPUBLIC

1.	Name of entity and common abbreviation	Spoločnost's ručenim obmedzením (s.r.o.)	Verejná obchodná spoločnost' (v.o.s)	Komanditná spoločnost'[1] (k.s.)
2.	English translation	Limited liability company	General partnership	Limited partnership
3.	Does the entity file a tax return?	Yes	No	Yes
4.	Is tax on the income of the entity assessed on the entity itself?	Yes	No	Yes
5.	Is the tax which is imposed on the income of the entity as it arises a liability of the entity or a liability of the members?	The company	The partners	Both the partners and the entity
6.	If the tax is paid by the members, how is the income classified for tax purposes?	-	Business income	Business income
7.	Is the rate and type of tax applicable to the entity's income determined on the basis of the members?	No	Yes	Yes
8.	Is tax imposed on the recipient when the income of the entity is distributed to its members etc.?	Yes	No	Yes
9.	If the answer to 8 is yes, how is that income classified for tax purposes?	Dividends		Dividends
10.	Does your country consider the entity as a "company" for purposes of tax treaties?	Yes	No	No
11.	Do you consider the entity a "resident" for purposes of tax treaties?	Yes	No	No

NOTES (SLOVAK REPUBLIC)

1. The tax base of the limited partnership is divided among its general partners and limited partners. The income of general partners is taxed as business income in the hands of these partners. The general partner must include this income in his income tax return. The income of limited partners is taxed as business income of a company. The income shared by the general partners is deducted from the tax base of the company.

SPAIN

1.	Name of entity and common abbreviation	Sociedad Colectiva	Sociedad Comanditaria	Sociedad Anónima
2.	English translation	General partnership	Limited partnership	Company limited by shares
3.	Does the entity file a tax return?	Yes	Yes	Yes
4.	Is tax on the income of the entity assessed on the entity itself?	Yes	Yes	Yes
5.	Is the tax which is imposed on the income of the entity as it arises a liability of the entity or a liability of the members?	The company	The company	The company
6.	If the tax is paid by the members, how is the income classified for tax purposes?		-	-
7.	Is the rate and type of tax applicable to the entity's income determined on the basis of the members?	No	No	No
8.	Is tax imposed on the recipient when the income of the entity is distributed to its members etc.?	Yes	Yes	Yes
9.	If the answer to 8 is yes, how is that income classified for tax purposes?	Dividend	Dividend	Dividend
10.	Does your country consider the entity as a "company" for purposes of tax treaties?	Yes	Yes	Yes
11.	Do you consider the entity a "resident" for purposes of tax treaties?	Yes	Yes	Yes

APPLICATION OF THE MODEL TAX CONVENTION TO PARTNERSHIPS

SPAIN

1.	Name of entity and common abbreviation	Sociedad limitada	Sociedad civil
2.	English translation	Limited company	Civil law partnership
3.	Does the entity file a tax return?	Yes	No
4.	Is tax on the income of the entity assessed on the entity itself?	Yes	No
5.	Is the tax which is imposed on the income of the entity as it arises a liability of the entity or a liability of the members?	The company	The partners
6.	If the tax is paid by the members, how is the income classified for tax purposes?	-	Fiscal nature unchanged
7.	Is the rate and type of tax applicable to the entity's income determined on the basis of the members?	No	-
8.	Is tax imposed on the recipient when the income of the entity is distributed to its members etc.?	Yes	No
9.	If the answer to 8 is yes, how is that income classified for tax purposes?	Dividend	-
10.	Does your country consider the entity as a "company" for purposes of tax treaties?	Yes	No
11.	Do you consider the entity a "resident" for purposes of tax treaties?	Yes	No

SWEDEN

1.	Name of entity and common abbreviation	Handelsbolag (HB)	Kommanditbolag (KB)	Aktiebolag (AB)
2.	English translation	General partnership	Limited partnership	Limited company
3.	Does the entity file a tax return?	Yes	Yes	
4.	Is tax on the income of the entity assessed on the entity itself?[1]	No	No	Yes
5.	Is the tax which is imposed on the income of the entity as it arises a liability of the entity or a liability of the members?	Each partner	Each partner	The company
6.	If the tax is paid by the members, how is the income classified for tax purposes?[2]	Business profits	Business profits	-
7.	Is the rate and type of tax applicable to the entity's income determined on the basis of the members?	Yes	Yes	-
8.	Is tax imposed on the recipient when the income of the entity is distributed to its members etc.?	No	No	Yes
9.	If the answer to 8 is yes, how is that income classified for tax purposes?	-	-	Dividends
10.	Does your country consider the entity as a "company" for purposes of tax treaties?	No	No	Yes
11.	Do you consider the entity a "resident" for purposes of tax treaties?	No	No	Yes

NOTES (SWEDEN)

1. The total taxable income is computed at the level of the partnership. However the tax is assessed on each partner separately on the basis of his share of the partnership income and the partner is responsible for his own tax.

2. Where part of the activity of the partnership is in the nature of business then the entire partnership income will be classified as "business profits".

SWITZERLAND

1. Name of entity and common abbreviation	Gesellschaft mit beschrankter Haftung (GmbH)	Kollektiv-gesellschaft (Co, Cie)	Kommandit-gesellschaft (Co, Cie)	Einfachege-sellschaft
2. English translation	Limited liability company	General partnership	Limited partnership	Civil law partnership
3. Does the entity file a tax return?	Yes	No	No	No
4. Is tax on the income of the entity assessed on the entity itself?	Yes	No	No	No
5. Is the tax which is imposed on the income of the entity as it arises a liability of the entity or a liability of the members?	The company			
6. If the tax is paid by the members, how is the income classified for tax purposes?	-			
7. Is the rate and type of tax applicable to the entity's income determined on the basis of the members?	-			
8. Is tax imposed on the recipient when the income of the entity is distributed to its members etc.?	Yes	No	No	No
9. If the answer to 8 is yes, how is that income classified for tax purposes?	Dividend	-	-	-
10. Does your country consider the entity as a "company" for purposes of tax treaties?	Yes	No	No	No
11. Do you consider the entity a "resident" for purposes of tax treaties?	Yes	No[1]	No	No[1]

APPLICATION OF THE MODEL TAX CONVENTION TO PARTNERSHIPS

NOTES (SWITZERLAND)

1. Under specific provisions of Swiss Double Taxation Conventions the entity may be deemed to be a resident of Switzerland for the purpose of the Convention.

TURKEY

1.	Name of entity and common abbreviation	Anonim Şirket (AŞ)	Limited Şirket (Ltd/Ş)	Kollektif Şirket
2.	English translation	Joint Stock Company	Limited Liability Company	General partnership
3.	Does the entity file a tax return?	Yes	Yes	No
4.	Is tax on the income of the entity assessed on the entity itself?	Yes	Yes	No
5.	Is the tax which is imposed on the income of the entity as it arises a liability of the entity or a liability of the members?	The entity	The entity	The partner
6.	If the tax is paid by the members, how is the income classified for tax purposes?	-	-	Business income
7.	Is the rate and type of tax applicable to the entity's income determined on the basis of the members?	No	No	No
8.	Is tax imposed on the recipient when the income of the entity is distributed to its members etc.?	Yes	Yes	No
9.	If the answer to 8 is yes, how is that income classified for tax purposes?	Dividend	Dividend	-
10.	Does your country consider the entity as a "company" for purposes of tax treaties?	Yes	Yes	No
11.	Do you consider the entity a "resident" for purposes of tax treaties?	Yes	Yes	No

APPLICATION OF THE MODEL TAX CONVENTION TO PARTNERSHIPS

TURKEY

1.	Name of entity and common abbreviation	Adi Şirket	Eshamlı Komandit Şirket
2.	English translation	Partnership	Limited Partnership
3.	Does the entity file a tax return?	No	Yes
4.	Is tax on the income of the entity assessed on the entity itself?	No	Yes
5.	Is the tax which is imposed on the income of the entity as it arises a liability of the entity or a liability of the members?	The partner	The entity
6.	If the tax is paid by the members, how is the income classified for tax purposes?	Business income	Business income or dividends[1]
7.	Is the rate and type of tax applicable to the entity's income determined on the basis of the members?	No	No
8.	Is tax imposed on the recipient when the income of the entity is distributed to its members etc.?	No	Yes
9.	If the answer to 8 is yes, how is that income classified for tax purposes?	-	Dividend
10.	Does your country consider the entity as a "company" for purposes of tax treaties?	No	Yes
11.	Do you consider the entity a "resident" for purposes of tax treaties?	No	Yes

NOTES (TURKEY)

1. Income derived by partners with unlimited liability is deemed to be business income and income derived by partners with limited liability is deemed to be dividends.

APPLICATION OF THE MODEL TAX CONVENTION TO PARTNERSHIPS

UNITED KINGDOM

1.	Name of entity and common abbreviation	Limited Liability Company (Ltd/Plc)	Unlimited Company	Unincorporated Association
2.	English translation			
3.	Does the entity file a tax return?	Yes	Yes	Yes
4.	Is tax on the income of the entity assessed on the entity itself?	Yes	Yes	Yes
5.	Is the tax which is imposed on the income of the entity as it arises a liability of the entity or a liability of the members?	The entity	The entity	The entity
6.	If the tax is paid by the members, how is the income classified for tax purposes?			
7.	Is the rate and type of tax applicable to the entity's income determined on the basis of the members?	No- Same for all income of entity	No- Same for all income of entity	No- Same for all income of entity
8.	Is tax imposed on the recipient when the income of the entity is distributed to its members etc.?	Yes	Yes	Yes
9.	If the answer to 8 is yes, how is that income classified for tax purposes?	Dividend	Dividend	Dividend
10.	Does your country consider the entity as a "company" for purposes of tax treaties?	Yes	Yes	Yes
11.	Do you consider the entity a "resident" for purposes of tax treaties?	Yes	Yes	Yes

UNITED KINGDOM

1. Name of entity and commonly used abbreviation	Industrial & Provident Societies (IPS)	Ordinary Partnerships	Limited Partnerships
2. English translation			
3. Does the entity file an income tax return?	Yes	No	No
4. Is tax on the income of the entity assessed on the entity itself?	Yes	No	No
5. Is the tax which is imposed on the income of the entity as it arises a liability of the entity or a liability of the members?	The entity	The partner	The partner
6. If the tax is paid by the members, how is the income classified for tax purposes?		Fiscal nature unchanged	Fiscal nature unchanged
7. Is the rate and type of tax applicable to the entity's income determined on the basis of the members?	No - Same for all income of entity	Rate determined in relation to each partner	Rate determined in relation to each partner
8. Is tax imposed on the recipient when the income of the entity is distributed to its members etc?	Yes	No	No
9. If the answer to 8 is yes, how is the income then classified for tax purposes?	Dividend	-	-
10. Does your country consider the entity as a "company" for purposes of tax treaties?	Yes	No	No
11. Does your country consider the entity as a "resident" for purposes of tax treaties?	Yes	No	No

APPLICATION OF THE MODEL TAX CONVENTION TO PARTNERSHIPS

UNITED STATES

1. Name of entity and commonly used abbreviation	Corporation[1] (including federal or state law corporations, publicly traded partnerships, insurance companies, and banks)	Partnership[2]
2. English translation		
3. Does the entity file an income tax return?	Yes	Yes
4. Is tax on the income of the entity assessed on the entity itself?	Yes	No
5. Is the tax which is imposed on the income of the entity as it arises a liability of the entity or a liability of the members?	The entity	The partners
6. If the tax is paid by the members, how is the income classified for tax purposes?	-	Retains its fiscal nature
7. Is the rate and type of tax applicable to the entity's income determined on the basis of the members?	No	Yes
8. Is tax imposed on the recipient when the income of the entity is distributed to its members etc?	Yes	No
9. If the answer to 8 is yes, how is the income then classified for tax purposes?	Dividend	-
10. Does your country consider the entity as a "company" for purposes of tax treaties?	Yes	No
11. Does your country consider the entity as a "resident" for purposes of tax treaties?	Yes	Income, profit or gain is treated as derived by a resident only to the extent the partners are residents

UNITED STATES

1. Name of entity and commonly used abbreviation	S Corporation	Real Estate Investment Trust (REIT), and Regulated Investment Company (RIC)
2. English translation		
3. Does the entity file an income tax return?	Yes	Yes
4. Is tax on the income of the entity assessed on the entity itself?	No	Yes[3]
5. Is the tax which is imposed on the income of the entity as it arises a liability of the entity or a liability of the members?	The members	The entity
6. If the tax is paid by the members, how is the income classified for tax purposes?	Retains its fiscal nature	-
7. Is the rate and type of tax applicable to the entity's income determined on the basis of the members?	Yes	No
8. Is tax imposed on the recipient when the income of the entity is distributed to its members etc?	No	Yes
9. If the answer to 8 is yes, how is the income then classified for tax purposes?	-	Dividend or capital gain
10. Does your country consider the entity as a "company" for purposes of tax treaties?	Yes	Yes
11. Does your country consider the entity as a "resident" for purposes of tax treaties?	Income, profit or gain is treated as derived by a resident only to the extent the members are residents[4]	Yes

128

APPLICATION OF THE MODEL TAX CONVENTION TO PARTNERSHIPS

NOTES (UNITED STATES)

1. General partnerships, limited partnerships, limited liability companies (LLC), limited liability partnerships (LLP), trusts engaged in business activities, and other entities not explicitly included in the list of corporations may elect to be taxed as either a corporation or a partnership.

2. See footnote 1.

3. However, a deduction is allowed for dividends paid.

4. All members of an S Corporation must be either U.S. citizens or resident alien individuals (as determined under internal law).

OECD PUBLICATIONS, 2, rue André-Pascal, 75775 PARIS CEDEX 16
PRINTED IN FRANCE
(23 99 52 1 P) ISBN 92-64-17077-4 – No. 50827 1999